AMELIA EARHART

AMELIA EARHART

CAROL A. PEARCE

Facts On File Publications
New York, New York ● Oxford, England

To these heroes:
Robert Theodore Worthington
Edna and Wallace Pearce
Edna and Reverend Robert Washington

And to all for whom the band does not play

AMELIA EARHART

Copyright © 1988 by Carol A. Pearce

All photographs that appear in this book are courtesy of the
Smithsonian Institution, National Air & Space Museum.

Library of Congress Cataloging-in-Publication Data

Pearce, Carol A.
  Amelia Earhart

  (Makers of America)
  Bibliography: p.
  includes index.
  Summary: Traces the life of the pilot who, among other
achievements, became the first woman to fly across the
Atlantic Ocean.
  1. Earhart, Amelia, 1897-1937. 2. Air pilots—United
States—Biography [1. Earhart, Amelia, 1897-1937.
2. Air pilots] I. Title. II. Series: Makers of
America (Facts On File, Inc.)
TL540.E3P42 1988   629.13′092′4 [B] [92]   87-9102
ISBN 0-8160-1520-1

Series design: Debbie Glasserman

Printed in the United States of America

10 9 8 7 6 5 4 3 2 1

CONTENTS

ACKNOWLEDGMENTS

WITH SPECIAL THANKS TO:

Margaret and Ben E. Haller
Andrew Manshel, Esquire
Volunteer Lawyers for the Arts
William Deerfield
Anthony Scott
The Smithsonian Institution
Faye Gillis Wells
Merrill Scherr and the *New York Post*
Pat Riley, Teterboro Aviation Hall of Fame
Sam Flores
Purdue University Libraries
The Ninety-Nines, Inc.
U.S. Department of Transportation, Federal Aviation
    Administration
Muriel Earhart Morrissey

1

CRACKUP
First Round-the-World Attempt—1937

> It's amazing how much can happen
> in a dawn.
>
> Amelia Earhart

February 1937. A large map hung at the front of the Barclay Hotel room in New York City where the news conference took place. Amelia Earhart, aviator extraordinaire, strode to the front wearing a simple dark blue dress.

By this time, reporters took for granted her unassuming style, her modest manner, her sandy short-bobbed hair that always looked as though it needed a good brushing, her good-natured grin, the serious blue eyes. Medium height, she appeared taller because she was slender and had long legs.

"A Peter Pan figure," her husband, George Putnam, fondly observed.

Her appearance was a cross between handsome and pretty, though she considered herself unattractive. She and Eleanor Roosevelt, wife of President Franklin Roosevelt, both felt this way about themselves. It was one of the opinions they had in common and they had become friends during the course of Amelia's fame.

Speaking softly, Amelia traced out her planned route on the giant map. As her long graceful fingers moved on, she did not speak of fears or feelings at all, only of the trip she planned to make in a few months time.

"I'm going to fly around the globe," she announced. "The flight will be as near to the equator as I can make it, east to west, about 27,000 miles."

That itinerary would start out at Oakland, California, and continue to Honolulu, Hawaii; from there to Howland Island in the South Pacific; to Australia; India; Africa; Brazil; then on to New York.

The room was charged with the excitement of her announcement, though many had speculated that it was coming. Really, at this point there was nothing left for her to do BUT go around the world. This was one trip, one sojourn yet to be accomplished by any man or woman in an airplane.

In answer to a question from Carl Allen of the *New York Herald Tribune* as to the why of her decision, Amelia Earhart

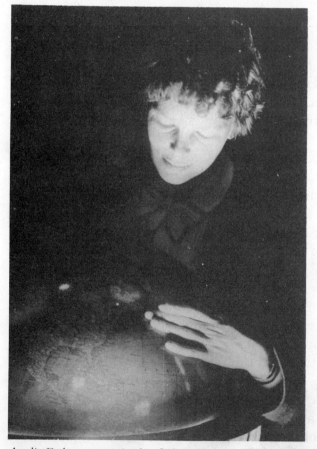

Amelia Earhart announcing her flight around the world, 1937

answered, "I'm getting old [she was 39] and want to make way for the new generation before I get feeble."

Another reporter, unable to grasp Amelia's reasoning, attempted to pin her down again: "Why do you want to make such a dangerous and exhausting flight?"

"Well, I've seen the North Atlantic [a reference to her earlier, historic, and record-breaking flight], and I've seen the Pacific, too, of course. Well—just say I want to fly around the globe at its waistline."

Over and over she would tell people that she wanted to make a particular flight simply because she wanted to do it—or because it was "fun." Critics picked up on the word "fun" and hounded her in print about it, saying, "Enough fun, Amelia, enough!" That, of course, only made her more determined than ever.

"One must take chances," she said calmly. To her, taking chances made her feel most alive. Women, she believed, were brought up to be much too timid.

Besides that, the sky is where she felt at home, felt free and whole. Her soul lay in the air. This was where she came closest to what she thought God must be. And though a private person who really hated the glare of the limelight, she kept doing the dangerous and the challenging that made her a public figure.

In addition, it was of utmost importance to her to prove over and over to an unbelieving world that women could do anything that men could. "There are economic, political, scientific, and artistic frontiers of the most exciting sort awaiting faith and the spirit of adventure to discover them," she said in her speeches.

The world was the last frontier to be conquered by air. Other pilots had been making extended trips. To stay ahead of them, Amelia Earhart had to do something dramatic.

Wiley Post, a friend of hers, flew around the world at the northern part in 1931 and again in 1933. The distance he covered was two-thirds the length she would travel, however. In 1935, he took off on a similar trip, this time carrying the popular actor and humorist Will Rogers as a passenger. They crashed on takeoff and both men were killed.

Charles and his wife, Ann Morrow Lindbergh, flew 29,000 miles in 1933, surveying Europe, Africa, and South America.

In 1934, Laura Ingalls soloed New York to South America and back for a total of 16,897 miles. Record breaking had turned into a numbers game by 1937.

At the same time, commercial flights had proliferated to the point where Pan Am Clipper ships were transporting passengers between San Francisco and Hong Kong. England's Imperial Airways flew a regular route to Egypt, India, and the Far East. Air France and KLM covered Southeast Asia.

To outdo her commercial and "amateur" competitors, Amelia Earhart, first woman of the air, had to do something requiring consummate skill and courage. The sole possibility was a complete circumnavigation of the world, stopping only at night to sleep.

Nearby that map in the Barclay Hotel stood Harry Manning, ship's captain with American President Lines. Amelia introduced him as her navigator for the first part of the trip. This was a surprise to reporters. Before, she had always gone solo, except, of course, for *The Friendship* flight, her first appearance on the aviation scene.

Manning, in fact, had been her friend since she sailed home on the ship he commanded, the SS *President Roosevelt*, after *The Friendship* flight across the Atlantic, a flight that etched her name forever in American history, making her the first woman to cross that ocean by air. On board the *Roosevelt*, she was besieged by curious passengers. To escape the attention, she spent time on the ship's bridge, where Manning gave her rudimentary instruction in celestial navigation, and they became friends.

Out of that friendship came a vow that one day they would fly together. His standing beside her that February day in 1937 as she made her historic annoucement was a result of that vow. On this biggest of all trips in her nine-year flying career, she wanted him along; so Manning took a leave of absence from his job and was ready to go.

He was eminently qualified for the backup spot. A congressional Medal of Honor winner, having rescued 32 men from a sinking ship off the coast of Florida, Harry Manning was a pilot and a navigator as well as a ship captain, skilled in Morse Code and celestial navigation. He could also operate a ham radio.

Why would she take a man along this time? The answer to that lay in the danger of the trip itself. She would have to find her way over thousands of miles of open ocean. There would be no room for mistakes, no chance to come down and ask directions. She was taking Manning along to help her over the "rough spots," which mostly involved the South Pacific passage. Even the independent Amelia Earhart had to acknowledge that sometimes she couldn't do everything alone.

After talking over the trip, in the conception stages the previous year, she and her husband, George Putnam, had concluded that she would need a good navigator for at least part of the way. Harry Manning was not their first choice.

George Putnam first recommended Bradford Washburn, Jr. At 26, Washburn headed Harvard University's Institute of Geographical Exploration. He had led expeditions. He was a flier, a photographer, and an expert at navigation, which he taught at Harvard. In the circle of explorers and adventurers in which Amelia and GP traveled, Bradford Wasburn was highly praised. So they invited him to dinner at their house in Rye, New York. They wanted to take his measure, sound him out, and see if Amelia might want to invite him along.

Over dinner, she casually brought up the topic of the trip she intended to make and for a while they discussed it without any mention of a potential role in it for Washburn, though he must have realized that they hadn't invited him to dinner without some good reason. Talking over the route, he picked out Howland Island as a subject of intense questioning. Howland was and is barely a pinprick in the vast Pacific Ocean.

How did Amelia expect to find it? Surely not by dead reckoning (compass bearings with provisions made for wind factor) alone? At that rate, if she were off course by so much as one degree, Washburn pointed out, she would miss the island entirely. Then what? In that part of the world, there would be no alternative landing sites in the event that she missed her primary target. Would there be radio direction signals coming from Howland itself?

No, she told Washburn. There would be no radio signals. Will you have direction-finding equipment on board the plane? he asked.

No. She didn't think such equipment was necessary.

For Washburn, the "interview" was over, and his manner no doubt conveyed his disinterest in the trip because he was never asked to be Amelia Earhart's navigator. And if he had been asked, he later said, he would have refused. "Her belief in her own flying abilities was towering," he said, but he wanted no part of this particular trip.

If Washburn wanted no part of any possible flying disaster, the public at large was also getting tired of hearing about such disasters, about aviators lost or killed in aerial adventures of the sort Amelia Earhart regularly undertook. By 1937 editorials had already begun appearing in newspapers stating that there was nothing to be gained by such chancy expeditions, except perhaps to boost the self-confidence of the pilot.

The government had started to discourage such risk taking as well. "There's no more room for heroes in flying" was actually one airline's slogan.

The times were changing rapidly and with them attitudes toward flying adventures. The window of time was closing on Amelia Earhart.

That's why her announcement in the newspapers didn't generate the excitement it might have in years past. Planes had become familiar sights in the sky, rather than strange and unusual objects. Whereas once whole families would drive to dusty airfields on Sundays in order to mingle with huge crowds that gathered to watch aviators take off, stunt, and land; whereas once schools would cancel classes when a barnstormer alighted in a field near town so that everybody, including the children, could turn out to watch him fly and perhaps take a ride for a dollar (the pilot was inevitably a man then); now that romance was gone. People were used to the idea of aviation. Many women were flying; young people were learning to fly; businessmen flew as passengers; mail was routinely flown. The newness, the thrill were gone.

Privately, perhaps some part of Amelia Earhart was ready for a change, too. After this trip, she confided to friends, maybe she would retire from long-distance "stunt" flying. Maybe she'd spend some time writing poetry—or perhaps screenplays. She had always enjoyed writing and dabbled in it when she could grab a few minutes. Maybe she'd do some of the things she'd literally had no time to do before. Maybe she'd slow down and begin to enjoy some of the pleasures of life as well.

The year before, on July 24, 1936, Amelia Earhart's 39th birthday, she had taken possession of the airplane she would use to take her around the world. It was an all-metal twin-engine Lockheed Electra (named after the "lost" star of the Pleiades) with retractable landing gear and a 55-foot wingspan, capable of speeds up to 210 mph and 27,000-foot altitudes. It represented the state of the art in aviation equipment.

It had cost $80,000 during a time when the Great Depression still had people on bread lines, in soup kitchens, and, if they were lucky, in government work projects. Purdue University bought it for her: she termed it her "flying laboratory."

Purdue was one of the few universities to have its own airfield, and for the past year, Amelia worked there part time as women's career counselor and aviation consultant. She relished the chance to give her opinions to young women starting out in their lives, to encourage them to follow their dreams as she had. And perhaps, too, this airplane had been part of the deal from the beginning.

Years later, Purdue's dean of engineering, Audrey Potter, told CBS newsman Fred Goerner that U.S. government funds were involved in the purchase of Amelia Earhart's Electra airplane. He wrote Goerner that the money had been channeled through two private individuals, and from them into the Purdue Research Foundation, which paid for the plane. The understanding was, he said, that she would assist in the development of direction-finding equipment, which was a top-secret field at the time.

Today no one is sure exactly what changes were made on the airplane before takeoff. What is known is that the seats were removed so that extra fuel tanks could be added. This was standard procedure for someone preparing to make a trip as long as the one Amelia intended. Clarence Belinn, a friend of Amelia's and her husband, and superintendent for National Airways, designed the auxiliary tank system so that it would be possible for her to fly long distances without stopping. When he was done, the Electra had a newly outfitted 1,200-gallon fuel capacity, which gave it a cruising range of up to 4,000 miles.

(Telling no one at the time, Belinn held the private opinion that Amelia Earhart was living on borrowed time. After her Atlantic solo in 1932, he had gone over the Lockheed Vega she used in the flight. Four of the brackets attaching one wing to the fuselage were cracked to the point of yield.)

What is also known is that a navigation area was arranged in back of the bulkhead. This is where Harry Manning would spend his time during the long hours of flight. A chart table was bolted down. A window was outfitted with a pelorus for taking bearings from landmasses. It is believed that both Amelia and her navigator in the back of the plane had access to voice radios for transmitting and receiving, but they could not use these radios to communicate with each other. That would be handled by way of a bamboo fishing pole attached to the ceiling. Notes would be clipped to a line and reeled back and forth. Only the navigator had the telegraphic key for transmitting and receiving Morse Code messages. Amelia had no use for this key anyway. She did not know Morse Code and made no attempt to learn.

A technical expert had been hired during 1936 to oversee the flight and to make sure Amelia's skills were honed to the point where she could handle whatever came up along the way. The expert was Paul Mantz, who owned a flying service and was also a fine pilot. It was his idea to install certain expensive equipment, such as the Sperry Robot Pilot, which could be used to take over the controls on long hauls, letting Amelia relax and write in her log. Pilot fatigue was one of Mantz's main worries from the start.

To date, Amelia Earhart's solo records had all been set in single-engine planes, so she had to undergo extensive retraining on the large, twin-engine Electra. Mantz worked with her on this and on her instrument-handling capacities, which he wanted to see more disciplined and precise, so that she could fly "blind" whenever weather conditions necessitated. At the same time he oversaw the modifications to the airplane.

Amelia Earhart had learned to fly at a time when pilots navigated by landmarks and railroad tracks in order to find their way. At times, she had landed in pastures to ask directions. On the upcoming trip, when she got to the Pacific, or over Africa, for instance, there would be no landmarks to guide her. Everything would have to be done by instruments and/or radio.

While Mantz worried about Amelia's skills and possible fatigue marring her judgment, Amelia's friends showed great concern about the decision to make this trip. Jacqueline Cochran, a well-known pilot herself at the time, particularly fretted about those stretches over water. She gave her friend a brightly colored kite to use as a marker in case she had to ditch at sea, along with a set of fish hooks, and a pocket knife.

Jacqueline Cochran was also not enthusiastic about Harry Manning as a navigator. Being a ship's captain, she argued, he would be unused to making navigational decisions at high speed, as was necessary in the air. Take him on a test flight, she urged Amelia. Go out over the ocean from Burbank, California; circle, then have him give directions back to the airport.

This is what they did. Following Harry Manning's directions, Amelia reached the California coastline more than 200 miles off course, somewhere between Los Angeles and San Francisco. This probably should have caused her to cancel their agreement, as a 200-mile error on the trip ahead could jeopardize her life.

Instead, Amelia Earhart chose a second man to come along as backup to Harry Manning.

This second man turned out to be Fred Noonan. Noonan, like Manning, was a trained pilot, and, in addition, was one of the world's best aerial navigators. He had crossed the Pacific many times mapping out Pan Am's routes to the Far East and Pacific. He did not know Morse Code as Manning did, but that wasn't considered so essential at the time they were flying.

Noonan was a fun-loving and handsome Irishman. He leaped at the chance to come along on Amelia Earhart's trip because he could get no other job. Pan American had fired him because of a bottle-a-day drinking habit. "Too great a risk," the company called him. When contacted, however, Fred Noonan told Amelia he had quit drinking.

She had been through enough experience with alcoholics, beginning long before with her father. She should have been wary of Noonan's assertion. However, it wasn't easy then to locate pilots—or navigators—who weren't hard drinkers. In the early days of flying, drinking went right along with the high risks and physical discomfort of the small open-cockpit airplanes. Then after planes became faster, safer, and more comfortable, the drinking, which seemed so much a part of aviation, simply continued.

Men with alcohol problems were not new to Amelia Aerhart, both on the ground and in the air. Like many children of alcoholics, she may have carried with her into adulthood a guilt over her father whom she had been unable to "save" from his drinking when she was a child. In her dealings with family, she demonstrated a strong desire to be in control, to take care of people and tell them what to do. Letters to her mother include instructions on how to dress, where to spend her summers, and how to spend the money she sent along. In hiring Noonan to assist on this round-the-world flight, Amelia Earhart may have been pacifying her inner demons as well as fulfilling more obvious needs for navigational accuracy.

"It's the deep down inside one must live with," Jacqueline Cochran finally concluded, seeing Amelia plunge on into the heart of this journey, which would not let her rest without her trying it. And the deep down inside of Amelia Earhart seemed to bid her go on, whatever the cost.

Cochran's husband, Floyd Odlum, invested in Amelia's last flight along with others; he had come to terms with his own wife's risk taking in the air. He believed there was a fine line between acting according to logic and according to emotions. Learning which urge was driving you was something everybody had to do for themselves. Nobody can draw that line for another, he said. As for Amelia, she would not reconsider her decision. "The time to worry is three months before a flight," she said. "Decide then whether or not the goal is worth the risks involved. If it is, stop worrying. To worry is to add another hazard."

During the year of preparation, 1936, Amelia gave over 150 lectures, campaigned for Franklin Roosevelt's reelection, and oversaw work on the California home she and George Putnam were completing. Since her first Atlantic flight in 1928 she had been in great demand as a speaker. Treating her like a protégée, Putnam coached her on what to wear, how to speak, and what to say. This became a chief way in which she financed these expensive flights.

Occasionally she relaxed at Cochran's and Odlum's ranch. Once while she was there, word came of a plane that had disappeared on a flight to Salt Lake City. Knowing of Cochran's alleged ESP abilities, Amelia asked, "Can you locate it?" Cochran described where the plane went down and Amelia took off to search for it. A heavy snowfall kept her from finding the downed craft. Later in the season when the snows melted, the aircraft was found where Jacqueline Cochran had said it would be. Another time an airliner went down on its way to Los Angeles. Again Cochran described the site, gave the number of dead and injured, and proved to be accurate on all counts.

In 1936, Amelia made short shakedown flights with the Electra, and during one, a fire started in one of the engines. She put it out, but the event was treated as news and reported over the radio. Before Cochran heard about the fire she knew it had happened. Much later she had reason to lament, "If my strange ability was worth anything, it should have saved Amelia."

Another pilot friend, Louise Thaden, flew to California hoping to talk Amelia out of the round-the-world flight. "Wait until you can afford the best radio equipment around," Thaden urged. Amelia told her, "I've always wanted to do this flight. If I should bop off, it will be doing the thing I wanted most to do. The Man with the little black book has a date marked down for all of us—when our work here is finished . . ."

When it came to taking chances, to bearing the burdens and the danger, women took no back seat to men in aviation.

Meanwhile George Putnam did what he did best: promoted the trip and raised money to fund it. He solicited contributions from airlines and friends. He sold Gimbels on the idea of mail covers to be sent back from various spots along the way, then peddled the idea to collectors. In this way he raised $25,000. Arrangements for fuel and mechanics had to be made for her planned stops. Painstakingly Putnam arranged credentials for her and the crew, visas for every country, passports, health certificates, negative police records. One entire month was spent going to embassies in Washington, D.C.

In her spare time, Amelia filled charts with information, noting things like prevailing winds, terrain, compass courses, altitudes of mountain ranges, and possible emergency landing sites.

One night in Brooklyn, she and George were driving home when an old man crossed the street before them. Amelia drove around the block to study the man again. Something in him had struck her. But when they got to the same spot, the man was gone. At home that night she told her husband, "I think I'll not live to be old."

That February news conference quickened the pace of preparation. Paul Mantz wanted Amelia to take a cross-country trip so that she could get more accustomed to the plane, but she didn't have time. She proposed that he fly the first hop with them, as far as Honolulu. That way she could do most of the flying, and he could give her pointers along the way. He agreed.

In early spring 1937, the flight was delayed several days due to bad weather. Then came March 17—St. Patrick's Day of 1937. Rain fell all that morning in Burbank. It turned to drizzle in the afternoon. Finally the sun shone.

The three men, Mantz, Manning, and Noonan, hurried to the airfield. Amelia and George Putnam drove over as soon as they knew the weather was clearing. It was time to go.

Technicians pulled the Electra out of the Burbank hangar at 4:00 P.M. Mantz sat at the controls. Manning and Noonan huddled in the navigation area in back. To avoid being spotted by wellwishers and reporters, Amelia waited in an official Navy car with G.P. until Mantz had taxied all the way to the end of the runway. Then she was driven out to the plane. Getting up onto a wing, she waved goodbye to her husband, then climbed aboard to take the controls.

For a full five minutes she revved the huge Wasp engine. At 4:30 P.M., the five-ton plane, heavy with gasoline, rumbled down the runway. Gradually it picked up speed, splashing through puddles that gleamed in the late afternoon sun. Its wheels lifted off the ground. Takeoff. The wheels were retracted. The round-the-world trip began.

As Amelia turned the Electra's nose to the west and Honolulu, Manning and Noonan busily plotted their course. Just after leaving the coastline of California, they encountered a Pan Am Clipper heading in. This was the very first airplane Amelia had ever seen in the air on one of her flights. The pilot was Ed Musick. This was his first encounter with another aircraft in flight as well.

Amelia flew 50 minutes out of each hour, then Mantz took over to give her a break. While she flew, he kept track of how quickly they were using fuel and also worked the radio. He managed to pick up stations at great distances without a problem. The plane worked beautifully as they flew on toward Hawaii and through the night.

The trip took over 15 hours. As they approached the range of the Makapuu radio beacon on Oahu, for the first time Amelia worked the radio loop antenna, which was fastened to the top of the cockpit roof, like the key in a windup toy. From her seat in the cockpit, she was able to rotate the loop to get a "null," or band of no sound, in her earphones. This indicated the direction of the beacon. With this information, she then turned the plane to a bearing on the beacon, allowing for course correction because of wind drift, a calculation Fred Noonan had sent up by note a few minutes earlier.

Meanwhile, in the back, Harry Manning worked the telegraph key, sending signals to Makapuu so that the station could, in turn, get its own bearing on the aircraft. However, something malfunctioned at this point and the telegraph generator burned out. Makapuu did not have enough time to take a bearing, so the Electra approached Honolulu carrying the three men and the most famous and perhaps the most beloved woman in the world aboard, without anyone knowing their exact location in the air.

Eighty miles out of Wheeler Field in Honolulu, Fred Noonan sent word to the cockpit: Begin descent. Amelia was tired from the all-night flight. She asked Paul Mantz to take the plane down.

This was something that only reinforced Mantz' notion that pilot fatigue could prove a critical factor in the long and arduous journey Amelia Earhart had to make from Honolulu. After this first hop, she was already tired. The incident haunted Mantz later.

Tired or not, she had to wave cheerily to hundreds of people who had gathered to celebrate her arrival. This had been the way she had to behave for years, ignoring her own feelings, putting on a good show for the crowds, smiling for photographers.

And tired or not, Amelia planned to move right on the same day. Only bad weather disrupted her plans. Through rain squalls, she and her crew drove to the home of Paul Mantz' friends Chris and Mona Holmes. There Amelia rested for the day, hoping for the skies to clear quickly. That evening the Holmes' threw a luau complete with hula dancers, but with much on her mind, the guest of honor, Amelia Earhart, left to walk alone on the beach.

Paul Mantz's fiancée was there to greet him. Once Amelia took off from Hawaii on her way westward, his work would be over, all but the worrying, so he planned to spend some time relaxing in Hawaii with his bride-to-be.

As for the other men, Fred Noonan would disembark at the first stop, which was Howland Island in the South Pacific, and Harry Manning would stay with the flight until Sydney, Australia. From there, Amelia would push on by herself.

She had always been a loner, but since fame caught up with her, she had become increasingly preoccupied and remote. She kept her own counsel and confided only in her husband and a few very close friends, such as Jacqueline Cochran.

As she pondered the world ahead of her that she hoped to traverse, and events and emergencies she had no way of anticipating on takeoff, the knowledge of her past experiences must have reassured her. She would do her best as it came to her to do, the way she always had. Once she admitted to her sister, Muriel, that she was occasionally scared, both before and during a trip. She never confessed that to anyone else. Perhaps as she walked the beach that night, looking at the dark clouds in the tropical sky, she thought of Muriel, who was talking to a lawyer about a divorce from her husband. When this trip ended, those problems would move to the forefront. Muriel might be bringing her two children to come to stay with Amelia and George Putnam.

"Human crises have a way of happening at inconvenient times," Amelia once said in her typically understated fashion.

"The girl in brown who walks alone," the caption under her high school yearbook photo read, and that evening she once again walked alone as she faced an uncertain future.

The next morning brought more storms. Paul Mantz moved the Electra to Luke Field, near Pearl Harbor. This facility provided a longer runway for the plane, which needed all the space it could get in order to leave the ground while loaded down with gasoline. Mantz oversaw the filling of the tanks with high-octane military fuel. There would be enough on board so that if Amelia and her companions didn't spot Howland Island, she could turn around and get back to Hawaii.

Howland would be that hard to find. Everyone was edgy about it. From the air, when and if she found it, the island would look like a dot of surf in water full of ripples and waves. How to distinguish it from the normal eddies and swirls in the Pacific was a big problem. Previously there had been no landing field there, but when Amelia made known her need for a place to refuel, the U.S. Department of Commerce, under President Franklin Roosevelt's directions, hauled equipment in by ship to level and grade a dirt runway sufficient to accommodate the Electra. By the time Amelia walked on the beach that March night in Hawaii, the field was ready; in addition, a Coast Guard ship, the *Itasca*, lay off the island to help guide her to it.

That day a Pratt and Whitney mechanic in Hawaii went over the airplane's engines, making sure they were operating properly. In response to improved weather forecasts, a departure date was set for March 20 (just one year from the date the Electra had been ordered from Lockheed). On that day, not only would conditions be favorable in Hawaii but also southwest to the Micronesia area where the plane would be headed.

Before the sun came up that fateful March day set for takeoff, Paul Mantz drove to the field. In the darkness, he checked over the plane, warming the engines. As the first faint strains of light touched the Pearl Harbor hills, Harry Manning, Fred Noonan, and Amelia Earhart arrived.

Army officers collected in small groups to watch. In that humid tropical dawn, as Amelia prepared to board her plane, Paul Mantz slipped a lei of paper orchids over her head, wishing her luck, reiterating one last warning, "Remember, don't jockey the throttles."

This was an easy mistake for someone used to flying single-engine craft as she was. Each engine responded differently, nevertheless the throttles had to be handled smoothly and steadily. Direction could not be safely corrected by playing one throttle off against the other.

The air smelled fresh from past days' rain. Puddles covered the airstrip, as they had for the California takeoff. Aboard, her engines roaring, Amelia waved for mechanics to remove chocks from the Electra's wheels; then the plane began to roll, taxiing slowly to the end of the runway.

From a ramp at the sidelines, Paul Mantz watched anxiously as a father with a favorite child. Everything proceeded smoothly. At the far end of the field, Amelia turned the plane and it remained poised as she revved the engines. The roar of the two 1,100-horsepower motors thundered in the quiet air. Under the staying hand of the slim, determined woman, the plane shuddered. Then it began to move.

It lumbered forward, moving slowly at first, ungainly with its enormous load of gasoline. Gradually the Electra picked up speed until, faster and faster, it ate up the rain-slicked runway until it was hurtling, just moments away from takeoff.

"So easily was the plane moving down the runway," Amelia commented later, "that I thought takeoff was actually over. In ten seconds more, we would have been off the ground, with our landing gear tucked up and on our way southwestward. There wasn't the slightest indication of anything abnormal."

The plane reached 50, 55, then 60 miles an hour. Just as it seemed about to lift off the ground, one wing dipped. The plane began to feel strangely light to Amelia.

Something was wrong.

Moving quickly, she reduced power on the opposite engine to try to correct the drift. The silver plane pulled to the right. A split second later, the nose swung to the left. The right wing would not lift. Its tip scraped the ground in a great shower of sparks. To those watching, the noise was sickening.

"DON'T JOCKEY THE THROTTLE," Paul Mantz screamed helplessly.

In the copilot's seat, Manning thought they were headed for the sea beyond the runway; then the next thing he knew they were heading straight for the hangars at full speed. "There was nothing I could do," he said. "I felt the gear going and I was ready to die."

Sparks flew like firework sprays as metal hit and scraped wet concrete. The plane swung out of control, skidding into a complete circle at high speed. The right landing gear wrenched free. Gasoline spewed in the air. Even as this happened, Amelia Earhart thought, "If we don't burn up, I want to try again." The whole crackup was over in 10 seconds. Amelia cut the ignition.

At the first sign of trouble, ambulances and fire trucks began to roar down the runway toward the plane. Paul Mantz took off running to where the Electra lay ominously still.

A badly shaken Harry Manning climbed out first. Then Amelia emerged, trembling and pale. "The airplane which brought us so gallantly to Honolulu, lay on the concrete runway a poor battered bird with broken wings," Amelia said later.

"I don't know what happened, Paul," she told Mantz.

Taking his time, Fred Noonan finally appeared, casually folding up his charts.

From a distance, they inspected the damage: a right wheel sheared off, right wing battered and bent along with the vertical stabilizer, gas leaking from the tank on the wing, both propellers and the landing gear wrecked. Fire trucks poured sand and chemicals onto the spouting gasoline, which could easily have exploded.

Then, dispiritedly, Amelia and her crew walked back toward the hangars.

"Will you try again?" newsmen shouted. "Will you give up the flight now?"

Sadly Amelia shook her head. "Of course not. I'll certainly try again." Perhaps inside she was not so sure.

Nobody ever found out what went wrong with that takeoff, though everyone had theories. Some observers believed that a tire blew. Paul Mantz thought that Amelia had jockeyed the throttles, and nothing could shake him from this opinion. Whatever had happened, Harry Manning thought the crash was her fault.

"What about your husband's feelings?" a reporter asked.

Since daybreak at the Oakland airport George Putnam had been waiting for word of his wife's takeoff. Then a call came from a reporter at the scene.

"Have you heard," the man yelled. "They crashed. The ship's in flames."

Putnam put down the phone and walked outside. Someone else had to hang up the receiver. A few minutes later another call came. This one contradicted the first message; it said that the first story was false, based on the sprays of fire when the plane crashed.

"The black wings brushed close again," Putnam later wrote in his book *Soaring Wings*.

At once he cabled his wife at Luke Field. As she spoke with reporters, his message arrived, so she read it to them.

> SO LONG AS YOU AND THE BOYS ARE OK THE REST DOESN'T MATTER. AFTER ALL IT'S JUST ONE OF THOSE THINGS. WHETHER YOU WANT TO CALL IT A DAY OR KEEP GOING IS EQUALLY JAKE WITH ME.

"I feel better than ever about the ship," Amelia stated firmly. "I am more eager than ever to fly again."

In Medford, Massachusetts, a call came for Amelia's mother, Amy. Grabbing a pencil and paper, Amy began to write: "Plane in full speed at the time. Amelia is alright, going to continue flight."

Before noon that March 20, Amelia arranged for the mail covers to be safely stored with the Honolulu post office; she signed papers to have her plane shipped to the Lockheed plant in California, and she, Manning, and Noonan climbed aboard the cruise ship *Malolo* heading for California.

"It's amazing how much can happen in a dawn," she said.

Thoughts of Howland Island and its problems receded far into the background for the time being. She had much to do in a short period in order to keep her plans alive for this most challenging of all her journeys.

Aboard the *Malolo*, Harry Manning backed out of any future attempts to conquer the world in her Electra. He wanted to get back to his ship, where he had control and command. To others, he portrayed Amelia Earhart as temperamental, stubborn, someone who liked to have her own way.

With Manning out of the picture, Amelia had no one left to rely on but Fred Noonan. She could still make the flight with one skilled person aboard. She just couldn't do it alone. Noonan had shown great calm under stress that morning. That was a quality she particularly liked.

Would he go on with her? Could she rely on him?

As the *Malolo* proceeded toward California, Fred Noonan outlined his situation with her. He needed this flight. He felt that after it was over his reputation in the aviation business would be repaired enough for him to start a flying school. He needed something like this flight to undo the damage done by Pan American's firing. However, George Putnam had warned him not to capitalize on the trip in any way. All the acclaim was to go to Amelia, nobody else.

She brushed that aside. "Oh that's just how George is. You and I are in this together. If you go, we face the dangers together, we share the rewards as well."

German poet and playwright Johann Wolfgang von Goethe wrote, "Boldness has genius, power and magic in it." Like all pioneers, Amelia Earhart made bold moves. On her second attempt to set a record by traversing the world at the equator, she would take along a navigator who did not know Morse Code. The person on whom she would depend to the point of entrusting her life to him was a supposedly reformed alcoholic.

He questioned her: Did she trust him? Believe in him?

Without flinching, she replied, "I believe in you."

The round-the-world flight was on again. All that had to be done at this point was fix the airplane that would take them.

2

GIRL OF THE PRAIRIE
Midwest, 1897–1916

> He [or she] who would voyage into
> the secret night, who would step off
> the edge of the earth because it is
> there, must clearly be made of the
> Right Stuff.
>
> Salman Rushdie

When Amelia was a child, the 1904 World's Fair opened in St. Louis, Missouri. Her father, Edwin Earhart, splurged $100 to take her and her sister, Muriel. By a fluke, they missed the Wright brothers. Wilbur and Orville Wright decided that conditions at the fair weren't right for their flying machine, so they did not try for the $100,000 prize offered for anyone who could make a 10-minute flight around the grounds. Balloons with gasoline engines went unchallenged that year. Unknowingly, seven-year-old Amelia missed seeing her first airplane.

However, she did ride an elephant and the ferris wheel, and she did see a roller coaster.

"Get up," she woke Muriel early the first morning they were back home in Kansas City. "Get up."

"Why?" Muriel asked.

"Because we're going to build a roly."

And build a "roly" they did, with the help of a neighbor boy who brought over his toolbox. Tracks were built of two-by-four planks. Roller skates were nailed to a shorter board for a rider to use, and Amelia, always being the brave one, pioneered the first trip from shed roof to the ground. She landed with a crash. Not bothering about a cut lip, she looked over their handiwork. "It's the end," she said. "It's fine till you get to the end, but it's the end that counts. Make the track longer. Level it out."

So they constructed an extension to their track, which this time carried her out onto the grass. Again she landed with a tumble, but an easier one than before. She shouted, "IT'S LIKE FLYING. IT'S LIKE FLYING."

Those qualities that brought Amelia Earhart to the edge of the earth, ready to take off, run through her childhood like currents in a stream. "There they all were," she said later, "weaving in and out here and there through the years before aviation and I got together."

Anyone who knew her as a child would have been surprised if she *hadn't* gone on despite the crash in Hawaii. Her husband, George Palmer Putnam, said of her, "Give up? She never did." When she wanted to do something, she analyzed the difficulties, corrected what she could, prepared for what she was able, and, despite problems, plunged on.

Amelia Mary Earhart came into the world on July 24, 1897, in Atchison, Kansas, at a time when the frontier aura of that place was vanishing. The Indians were all but driven off the Kansas plains into reservations. Except for a handful of dreamers, people in general believed that human beings would never fly. In fact, the notion that we might be able to rise into the air on anything machine-powered and heavier than a balloon was considered about as silly an idea as thinking that rain could fall up instead of down.

Amelia was three when an unknown Wilbur Wright wrote in a letter: "For some years I've been afflicted with the belief that flight is possible to man." In 1903, the Wrights made their first powered flight in a heavier–than–air craft. Amelia Earhart was six at the time. The same principles that allowed the Wright brothers' boxy, kite-like machine to stay aloft a few short minutes at Kitty Hawk, North Carolina, are the same basic ones that apply to aircraft today. But Kitty Hawk was a

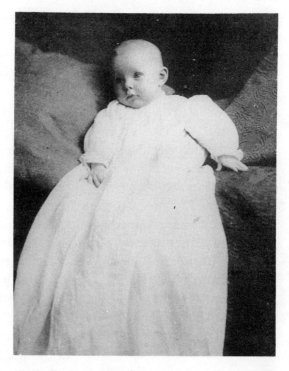

Amelia Earhart as an infant

long way from Atchison, Kansas, and Amelia did not see her first airplane in flight for another five years.

What *was* happening around her was that the world seemed to be desperately attempting to get off the ground. Gliders were slowly replacing gas-powered balloons. Engineless, they depended on good wind, good luck, and plenty of places to land when both gave out. If that wasn't dangerous enough, grown men were also doing things like jumping off barn roofs holding umbrella-like parachutes. Literally, an obsession with flying pervaded the country, and almost everyone with a speck of daring or adventure seemed afflicted by it.

Perhaps being the daughter of a railroad lawyer who frequently took her along on trips caused Amelia to fall in love with long distance. At the same time it made for an unsettled childhood. Not only was Edwin frequently away, but his income was also erratic, and meeting the bills, including the expenses for two young girls, put a strain on the family. So Amelia's mother, Amy, sent her and Muriel to stay with their grandparents in Atchison for most of their grade school years, while she and her husband continued to struggle along in Kansas City. In Atchison, she knew that the girls would have the best of everything, the comforts that had made her own childhood so smooth. The transition from being a pampered society belle to the wife of a claims lawyer for the railroad was made with many tears and much unhappiness, from which Amy shielded her daughters as much as possible.

As Muriel recalled, their father spent much of his time tinkering in the basement, inventing things that he hoped would make "their ship come in." While he dreamed of glory for himself and great luxury for his family, Edwin struggled to create something no one had ever thought up before.

One year he took money set aside to pay taxes and traveled to Washington, D.C., to patent one of his inventions. There he learned that the device had been invented by someone else two years before. The tax money was gone. This resulted in the selling of a set of law books given him by his wife's father, Judge Alfred Otis, something the Judge no doubt found unforgivable. It was either sell the books or lose their home.

As a result of Edwin's notions about ships coming in, his spending of the tax money on a gadget nobody wanted or needed, and his inability to keep up with his bills, the Otises, Edwin's in-laws, disliked him. From the beginning they had wanted their Amy to marry someone from her own social class. After all, they were one of the first families in Atchison, Kansas. Judge Otis, Amelia's grandfather, was one of the founders and first settlers of the town when it was a frontier stop for steamers on the Missouri River. Fresh out of the University of Michigan law school, Alfred Otis journeyed by stagecoach to Chicago, took a flatboat to St. Louis, and traveled up the Missouri River to stake his claim in Atchison. Then he sent for Amelia Harres to become his bride. Everything he touched turned to money.

He went on to become a district court judge, while at the same time he got rich in banking and land speculation. There was no better address than theirs—Quality Hill—a bluff overlooking the river. And this is where Amelia's mother, Amy, one of eight children, was raised to be a debutante. It was from this house, which has since been made into an Amelia Earhart museum, that Amy attended private school, rode horses from her parents' stables, and attended military balls at St. Joseph, traveling with a group of other young people by specially chartered steamer.

Fortune was not entirely kind to Amy Otis, however, and she had serious bouts of illness. Typhoid fever impaired her hearing when she was 16, and ever after that, when she was under stress, her hearing would worsen. Several years later, in 1889, as she was preparing to leave home to attend Vassar, she came down with diphtheria and nearly died. Almost miraculously, a young Atchison man who happened to be at home on a break from medical school, and perhaps the young man Judge Otis hoped his daughter might marry one day, saved her life by draining her lungs of fluid. Amy was nursed back to health by her 92-year-old grandmother, who had taken this duty on herself so that the rest of the family might avoid contagion. After a long convalescence, Amy gave up the idea of going away to school.

Nevertheless she remained active, teaching Sunday school, founding a Dickens Club, copying legal opinions for her father, and riding. Leader of a small Atchison social set, she was a popular, attractive young woman with a love for discussing current events. No doubt she had high expectations for her own future.

Since his favorite daughter was unable to attend school, and believing that trips were educational, Judge Otis took Amy along when he went West to investigate land offered for investment or as collateral on a loan. On one of these trips they joined with some sightseers ascending Pike's Peak. At a stage along the way, the women stopped to wait for the trip down, but Amy wanted to see the view from the top, so she kept going with the men. Only when she reached the pinnacle did she learn from rangers there that she was the first woman to climb all the way.

How the Otises must have regretted the day their son Mark brought Edwin Earhart home from the University of Kansas law school! Enthusiastic about his friend, Mark wanted Edwin to meet the family. It was the time of Amy's coming-out party, and the family's garden was decorated with flowers and paper lanterns. An orchestra played waltzes and the Virginia reel. The setting couldn't have been more romantic or more conducive to falling in love. This Edwin and Amy promptly did.

Edwin was from Atchison's "poor side" of town, Sumner, three miles south. He was shining shoes, tutoring, and tending furnaces to put himself through law school. He definitely hailed from the sod-hut class. But there he was, with his stern face, his whimsical humor, his poetic appreciation of that night's beauty, charming Amy more than any boy she had ever met.

Judge Otis saw red. Edwin Earhart was poor. Earhart's family always concerned itself, somewhat out of necessity, more with "moral riches" than material rewards, and misfortunes for them were practically a way of life.

Edwin's father, the Reverend David Earhart, a Lutheran evangelical minister, came West to settle at Sumner in the spring of 1860, around the same time as the Otises arrived. Their paths followed totally different courses from there. Reverend Earhart was equipped to teach Greek and Hebrew, not exactly essential subjects in frontier country. He founded three churches. The one nearest his home failed, but he kept the other two, one 50 miles away. He traveled to it every month without fail. At the same time, he tried to teach school and to raise enough food to feed his family. The year he arrived, drought struck, causing almost every crop to fail. The following year the Civil War broke out, and young men who might have been Rev. Earhart's students all left to join the fighting. At the same time grasshoppers destroyed every growing thing for two years running. Three years of war brought border fighting and runaway slaves, keeping things dangerously unsettled.

Through it all, "by teaching school and other secular labors." Rev. Earhart brought through his family of 12. Sometimes they ate nothing but turnips, but they did survive. He wanted Edwin, his youngest son, to become a preacher too, but Edwin wanted none of that, deciding instead to make his mark in the world as a lawyer.

After Amy Otis and Edwin Earhart met, Judge Otis tried every way he could to talk Amy out of her feelings for the gaunt, intense Earhart. Nothing worked. Once she set her mind on something, there was little anybody could do to change it. So the Judge set what he must have thought was an impossible condition for a man in Earhart's situation. Before he could marry Amy, he had to be earning at least $50 a month. The reason given by the Judge was that Amy needed to be provided for in the way to which she was accustomed. This was an enormous sum in a time when dresses cost $2, a chicken 25 cents, and bread a few pennies.

Edwin Earhart was equally determined on marrying the girl of his desire. After graduating from law school, he

Amelia's mother and father, Amy and Edwin Earhart, circa 1916, Kansas City, Missouri

worked out an arrangement with a railroad company whereby he would settle claims on a case-by-case basis. Quickly his income reached the Judge's $50 figure.

A man of his word, the Judge could not change his conditions at that point, so grudgingly the marriage plans went forward. On the excuse that a big affair would disturb Amelia's grandmother's tranquility, only the immediate families attended the small service in the fall of 1895. Two families were joined that day like oil and water—without mixing.

The bride wore a brown suit with leg-of-mutton sleeves and a bustle, a lacy blouse, a brown velvet hat, a marten fur muff and neck piece. The groom wore black tails. When the ceremony was over the couple left at once for Kansas City, Kansas, where a fully furnished home, bought for them by Judge Otis, awaited. There was no honeymoon.

Being away from her friends, her parents, everything that was familiar to her was very hard for the new bride. Then came an even harder event. Amy's first child was born dead.

The Otises no doubt blamed Edwin for that, too. It was two months before the baby was due, a hot, muggy August night in Kansas City. Edwin took Amy for a stroll, thinking an outing would cool them off before bed. Impulsively they took a cable car ride across the Kaw River. When the trip ended, Edwin jumped out to help Amy down, but the car jerked as she stood, and she fell hard against the brake lever. The next morning she gave birth to a stillborn infant—a girl.

Alone, carrying the child in a tiny coffin, Edwin Earhart brought it by train to Atchison, where it was buried in the Otis family's plot. This tragedy marred the start of their married lives together, and perhaps was an event from which neither of them fully recovered.

Shortly after the death of her first daughter, Amy became pregnant again. This time, the word went out from the Otis family: there would be no more accidents. Amy was to come home, where she could be properly looked after.

So it was in her grandparents' elegant Quality Hill home in Atchison, Kansas, that a healthy girl was born on July 24, 1897. She was christened Amelia Mary after her two grandmothers: Amelia Harres Otis and Mary Wells Patton Earhart. Quality Hill and the prairie finally joined in one wiry, curious, imaginative, poetic girl. Amidst dark-haired relatives, Amelia had a mass of blonde curls.

Three years later, Muriel Grace came along. The girls grew up pals. It wasn't until they were adults that they split off into entirely different directions. For now, life was good at Quality Hill. The sisters' nicknames for each other were Meely for Amelia and Pidge for Muriel. They made up imaginary friends, caught bugs, and kept them in boxes in their rooms after first identifying them from Amelia's *Insect Life* book. A pet mongrel dog, James Ferocious, added to their fun.

With her crinkly grin and bold spirit, Amelia led her playmates, including mostly Challis cousins from next door and Pidge. "Amelia was the most fun to play with," said her cousin Lucy Challis, often a fellow passenger on make-believe trips in the old carriage stored in the barn behind the Otis house.

James Stephens wrote, "How often we chase the thing that we ourselves become." Studying maps, which she loved, and which were brought from the house, Amelia played the game they named Bogie. They used real geographic terms for places to visit, and were always set upon along the way by wild bands of headhunters or thrashing crocodiles. Naturally they narrowly escaped with their lives, accompanied by much advice and chilling remarks from everyone aboard. "Isn't it about time we were getting to the next town?" one would say ominously. Or, "Let's see the map, this place doesn't look familiar to me." Or, "Anything might happen."

Said Lucy Challis, "I admired her [Amelia's] ability, stood in awe of her information, and loved her for herself—and it always held true."

Then there were the mud ball fights, the exploring of caves along the Missouri River bluffs. Any kind of strenuous game was most popular, including football, tennis, basketball, and bicycling. Amelia desperately wanted to learn to ride a horse, but Grandmother Otis said no, though her mother, Amy, had learned. Once Amelia climbed aboard a fat delivery horse by way of the shafts to his wagon harness. Then she couldn't get back down and had to be lifted. Still she "lived for the next experience of that kind."

She could jump higher than most boys in town, and when her grandmother saw her jump the picket fence rather than walk through the open gate, she lamented, "When I was your age I was content to do nothing more strenuous than roll a hoop in the town square."

When Amelia's father came to visit them, it was "war with the Indians," with Edwin playing the unlucky Indian. It's easy to believe that the Otises frowned on this sport as another example of Edwin Earhart's foolishness. The girls loved their father, though, and they especially loved his brand of play. Considering herself a "city girl," Amelia said she felt lucky to have any such foes as Indians to fight.

Edwin told them stories, too, primarily Western thrillers that would continue from one time to the next. Or he read aloud, so the girls learned to love reading and especially poetry. They recited poetry while they did housework, chanting things like "Horatius at the Bridge" or parts of "Sohrab and Rustum." Or one would read aloud while the other worked. Like most children, at one time Amelia thought her father knew everything there was to know. He would stump her with his use of huge words, which she then flew to look up in the dictionary. Once he wrote her a letter that began: "Dear parallelepipedon . . . "

"I was a horrid little girl . . . like many horrid children I loved school . . . perhaps the fact that I was exceedingly fond of reading made me endurable," said Amelia looking back on this period of her life. She read from the well-stacked shelves at the Otis home, graduating from children's books about boys and girls who "emerged triumphant over bad little boys and girls" to books by Sir Walter Scott, Charles Dickens, William Shakespeare, and Victor Hugo, as well as Oliver Optics Boys books. These latter irked her, though, because the heroes were always boys.

Luckily her parents were extremely open-minded for their day, and did not try to restrict her, or Muriel, just because they were girls. They were both encouraged to experiment, to try things, to do rather than hold back timidly. Nobody could

Muriel and Amelia Earhart, Atchison, Kansas, circa 1903

have been happier to take advantage of this freedom than Amelia Earhart.

The father of two girl friends owned a butcher shop, and sometimes when his horses weren't pulling the delivery wagon, the girls were allowed to ride. Naturally, Amelia was right there at those momentous times. The horses were old, but, she said, one "bucked with delightful determination for no reason at all. This horse opened vistas of pleasure for me."

By 1905 the Wright brothers were making extended flights with their boxy planes—up to 39 minutes in duration. And Amelia Earhart was already in love with the speed that would later draw her to flying.

For Christmas one year she asked for belly flop sleds of the kinds boys used, the ones with steel runners that were much faster than the girls' versions. Muriel asked for, and also got, a .22 gun; Amelia commented, "Muriel wheedled [the gun] on her own." They used it to shoot rats in the barn. The Otis handyman said that the barn came to look like a sieve before long. Many was the time Amelia was punished for coming late to dinner because she wouldn't give up waiting out a rat at his hole.

"Little girls shouldn't go around shooting," the Judge said, and the gun disappeared for a while. When it reappeared, the girls moved on to shooting bottles off the back fence. So Amelia knew those special rules for girls were there. And she was aware of the fact that boys were expected to be heroes, while little girls were expected to be pretty—and nice. It bothered her somewhat to be a maverick, to do things she knew were frowned on, but she took her major cues from her parents, and their attitude was: Life is the great teacher. Dealing with the new or the unknown is educational. Amelia Earhart followed this philosophy all through her life. She followed her desires relentlessly to know, to live, to seek out and to try what had not been tried before.

When her mother, Amy, cut up a chicken for supper, she turned it into a biology lesson for the girls, pointing out the various parts and naming them. Everything presented a chance to learn and to grow. And so, to Amelia, the world was full of fascinating things. She and Muriel were allowed to stay up late one night in 1910 to watch Halley's comet from the shed roof, and the comet put on a spectacular sky show.

Experimenting to see what would happen to radishes that weren't plucked when they were small, Amelia let hers grow to potato size, and named them Ear-dishes. They were too bitter to eat. Another time she let the weeds grow wild so she could see who would win—the radishes or the vegetables.

Sunday school was a weekly occurrence. It was from Bible readings that Amelia dreamed up her own version of manna. It had to be a cross between angel food cake and popovers, she was sure, but could never get the recipe to come out right. Later she said that if she ever gave up aviation, and had the time, she would perfect her "manna," knowing there would be quite a demand for it.

Her aunt, Margaret, Amy's sister, counted herself a loyal disciple of the famous suffragette Amelia Jenks Bloomer and made herself a Turkish-style dress (with bloomers), which was favored by suffragettes then. This inspired Amelia's mother to make her two girls bloomer-style gym suits for play. They were made of blue flannel with pleated bloomers that gathered at the knee and thus made tree-climbing a practical proposition. No longer were they held back in their activities by the usual dress with pinafores that little girls wore. Amelia admitted these outfits caused them to stand out as somewhat odd among their friends, none of whom deviated in their manner of dress from what was acceptable. But since the suits made it easier for her to outjump every boy in town, Amelia was content to wear them. That her girls were tomboys bothered Amy not at all. Those were happy days in Kansas for Amelia and Muriel.

In 1908 their father, perhaps urged by Amy to make a change for the better, took on a steady job with the Rock Island Railroad, which required that they move to Des Moines, Iowa. For a while the setup seemed ideal. The salary was good and it was regular. They bought a house. The girls could finally come to stay with their parents permanently, and none too soon, as Grandfather Otis was in bad health. When they left Atchison for Des Moines, Amelia was 11, Muriel 8. The change marked a turning point in their lives.

Their grandfather, David Earhart, had always bragged that nobody in their family ever touched a drop of liquor. However, Amelia's father, with visions of personal glory off in the vague future, found no challenges in going to work at the same job day after day. He got bored; he got discouraged. He began to drink.

Stopping to drink with friends after work turned into a habit. Then he began drinking during the day as well, and clerks began covering up his mistakes to save his job for him. The fear and worry this must have caused Amy was no doubt picked up by Amelia and Muriel.

Still there were some good times despite their father's unpredictability, bad temper, and odd behavior, which they didn't realize was the result of alcoholism. For Amelia's birthday, they attended the Iowa State Fair. She fussed with a paper hat that would not stay on her head, and paid little attention to a "thing of rusty wire and wood which looked not at all interesting." In it a man, wearing a helmet and goggles, sat on what looked like a box kite with sets of upper and lower wings, his feet on a bar. Somebody spun a propeller and a motor sizzled to life. This contraption rattled and bumped along in a field until it finally wobbled into the air. The blond-haired girl wearing the paper hat askew had known much more exciting journeys into the heartlands of Africa in her grandmother's worn-out carriage, and so paid little attention. Trying to elicit the proper awe and excitement, an adult pointed out to the impassive Amelia Earhart: "Look dear. It flies!"

Within the next two years the Wrights set flying records. Wilbur concentrated his efforts at the resort town of Pau in southern France, where he managed to spend up to two hours aloft at a stretch. Still, the fashionable set there much preferred horses, since going up into the air seemed more trouble than it was worth. Once up, where were you to go? Besides, a horse was reliable.

On July 25, 1909, Louis Blériot crossed the English Channel by plane. The record-setting, record-seeking days of aviation were launched in this one successful flight. Blériot returned to a thunderous hero's welcome in Paris. Suddenly tiny craft everywhere were taking to the skies like berserk dragonflies with sheer, fragile wings. Men began attempting stunts with these vehicles such as walking on the wings, dangling midair with their teeth chenched on a trailing rope, or leaping from one aloft plane to another. For a while, the unknown Charles A. Lindbergh would be a wing-walker in order to earn money to buy his own plane. But in 1909 he was merely seven years old, growing up like Amelia Earhart in the first flowering of flight.

People fell in love with planes and pilots, though they were still a rare sight, at the same time as they fell in love with speed, a love that characterized the Roaring Twenties.

Amelia's love of speed didn't slacken as she grew, either. From close calls on her sled, she went on to riding a pony in the summers she spent at Worthing, Minnesota, on Lake Okabena. This is when she really learned to ride, and since there was no saddle to be used, she wound up walking back from her trips into the woods at least half the time. No adventure for her was complete without such surprises.

The problems of her father's drinking continued. "Make do with cheerfulness," Grandfather Earhart always preached. This was what Amelia, her mother, and her sister were trying to do. Amelia's beloved father had, what her mother Amy called, "Dad's sickness." One night he was supposed to take Amelia and Muriel to a school dance. When he didn't get home after work, the girls sat waiting, trying not to wrinkle their good dresses or to get hot or impatient or angry or upset. When he finally got home, he shouted at them when they mentioned missing the dance. Muriel ran upstairs crying. Amelia simply climbed up the stairs, took off her dress, and hung it in the closet. There would be another time, she said, learning quickly to hide her feelings.

Another time, she found a hidden bottle of liquor and was just pouring its contents down the drain when her father caught her. Grabbing the bottle, he raised his arm to strike her but stopped at the last second. This, too, no doubt had a devastating effect on his older daughter.

Where before he loved to hear the girls quote poetry, now he wasn't interested. As often as three times a week he came home acting like a stranger. He took no notice of their accomplishments in school. Their mother's hearing worsened and she was always worried.

By 1911 both Otis grandparents were dead. The house at Quality Hill was sold at auction. Amy's share of the inheritance was withheld, to be given only after either 20 years had passed or Edwin Earhart died. The Otises believed Edwin squandered money, and they didn't want him to get his hands on their daughter's. Even in death, the Otises rejected Amelia's father; his drinking increased and became more frequent.

When at last a supervisor on Edwin's job learned the truth about his drinking, he told him that he had to go for a "cure" or he would lose his job. Edwin announced to the family that he was going away for a short while. A month at the Keely Cure Hospital must have upset his family as much as it did Edwin Earhart. There he was given drugs that made him sicken at even the smell of alcohol. He returned home swearing he would not touch another drop. Plans were made with great hopes for the future. He would take the girls fishing. They would have wonderful times again together.

Soon he was drinking as hard as ever. Then he was fired from his job. Searching everywhere for work brought no response. His reputation as a drinker spread throughout the railroad lines. The only work he found was a low-paying clerk's job in St. Paul, Minnesota. Sadly the family packed up their belongings and moved there. Though Otis relatives lived near the house they rented, they did not come to visit, and there was no money for entertaining, or for clothes, anyway.

Around this same time two women pilots blazed onto the aviation scene. Harriet Quimby and Blanche Scott struggled for the chance to participate in a field that men wanted to keep for themselves.

In a time when women were not allowed to serve on juries, hold public office, or vote, when property laws discriminated against them, when professions such as medicine and law were closed to them, when they didn't even have legal rights to their children, Blanche Scott and Harriet Quimby went knocking on doors asking for flying lessons. Even the Wright brothers turned Scott away. They wanted no part of teaching a woman to fly.

Persistence eventually paid off, though, and both women learned to fly. They blazed a trail that opened up the way for Amelia Earhart and others like her, and a glory beyond what they could possibly dream at the time.

One of their biggest problems sounds silly today. It was: What to wear? Men wore business suits with high starched collars. It was not so simple for women. Certainly the girdles and hoops and corsets, full skirts, and garters of the day didn't go with flying airplanes. Quimby and Scott had to devise a costume that would allow them to climb on the wing of an airplane and in and out of the cockpit with enough dignity to still be ladylike, since women definitely did not wear pants. Quimby made herself satin knickerbockers and wore high lace boots. Capes were used to cover what was then considered the shame of the knickers, since women were only supposed to wear long, full skirts. Sometimes their airplanes were sabotaged by outraged male pilots.

In 1912 flying pioneer Harriet Quimby was killed in a crash. The *Boston Post* wrote: "Anxious to be among the pathfinders, she took her chances like a man and died like one." From then until the early 1930s was a time of flying heroes.

The Earharts' heroism during this period was of a more quiet variety, and it involved living from one day to the next with an alcoholic. Edwin Earhart was hit by a car while getting off a streetcar in St. Paul. He wasn't critically hurt, but this incident, too, added to the terrible strain. Amelia was a junior in Central High in St. Paul, and in her free time she was selling rags, old iron, and bottles from the cellar to bring some money into the house. While she never cared for sewing, she pressed herself to invent ways to change dresses to make them look new, and sometimes cut up old curtains to make clothes for herself and Muriel.

In the spring of 1914, the family's hopes again rose. An offer of a job arrived. It was in a claims office in St. Louis, Missouri. Once more the family packed and left town. After a 10-hour train ride, they discovered there was no job. The man wasn't retiring from his post after all, or so Edwin was told. No doubt what had happened was that his reputation once again ruined his chances at a fresh start.

Weary now, homeless, disheartened, the family assessed its future, and Amy took hold. Edwin must go on his own. She would stay with friends while he tried to pull himself together. At that point, after losing what must have seemed his last chance for a good job, her decision must have been a terrible blow to Edwin. But how could he argue? What she said was true. The family, and probably most of all Amy, could tolerate no more stress as the result of his drinking problem. So many dashed hopes over the years, so many plans and dreams that never panned out, and then this. Amy needed to be free of the emotional burden at last. Edwin Earhart, unable to provide for his family, hit the lowest point of his life and he went to live with his sister in Kansas City,

Kansas. Amy took Amelia and Muriel to live with the Shedd family, friends in Chicago.

While Edwin attempted to set up a law practice in Kansas City, Amelia, who now loved science, went around interviewing at high schools to find one with a good science department. Hyde Park High suited her, so she enrolled there and Amy took an apartment nearby. Since AE showed so much independence of spirit by then in the choosing of a school, it's possible that she had also had something to say about their moving to Chicago. With the family split, she gradually assumed a leadership role that grew with the years until Amy and Muriel looked to her for support and guidance.

This same stubborn keeping of her own counsel, which would later strike some as temperamentalism, became one of Amelia's trademarks. By the time she was a teenager, she had learned not to look for answers anywhere but inside herself. These had been years of turmoil. Her father could not be saved by her love. She would now become a world to herself and stay aloof when it was possible.

"Amelia didn't feel safe anywhere," her mother said of the quiet, reclusive loner her daughter became before fame caught up with her. "And so she had to put on an outside." The mask that shielded her from caring too much and protected her feelings was formed long before fame came along.

"The girl in brown who walks alone" was the caption underneath her yearbook photo. Going it alone was one of Amelia's stellar characteristics by the time she reached high school.

Hyde Park High wasn't perfect, and Amelia tried to have an English teacher removed because the teacher, a political appointee, was incompetent. She failed but did win permission to spend her English periods in the library, where she could read what she liked. Graduation, on June 16, 1916, saw Amelia Earhart's name being called but no one showing up to claim the diploma. Citations, awards, prizes, diplomas meant little to her. All that mattered was that after attending six high schools, she nonetheless managed to graduate in four years. If she accomplished what she set as her goal, then the approval of others had little effect on Amelia Earhart.

One of her early school teachers, Miss Sarah Walton, said of her, "Amelia's mind is brilliant but she refuses to do the plodding necessary to win honor prizes."

A plodder she wasn't. But she was a believer. From the time she was very young, she believed that girls "can," in a world where people deeply held that "girls don't" and "girls can't."

Her childhood years also showed that change didn't seem to daunt her. "I never lived more than four years in any one place," she said when a stranger asked what her home town was. In fact, Amelia Earhart encouraged herself and those around her to seek change, to experiment. "I think the most important thing any girl can do is try herself out. Do something. You find the unexpected everywhere . . . by adventuring you become accustomed to the unexpected. The unexpected then becomes what it really is—the inevitable."

It would have been impossible for anyone, seeing her emerge from high school in Chicago, to predict that Amelia Mary Earhart would move on from there to become one of history's heroes. Who could have known then that, through aviation, she would challenge men's domains of adventure, business, aviation, power, and fame, and claim a part of their pie for herself and for women in general? Who could have known in an era when women were raised to eventually take their place behind the scenes at home—raising children, cooking meals, cleaning—that she would turn her back on all that and blaze a trail into uncharted territory? Who could have known in a day when cooking and sewing skills were the primary ways in which a woman's worth was judged—that and pleasing a man with beauty and charm—Amelia Earhart would dare the world to consider her as a capable, intelligent, sensitive, and sensible human being.

While some women marched and rallied and pleaded to be given the vote, she went on with her life, behaving as though she had always had all the rights she wanted. Be, do, try, those were her mottos. And in her unwillingness to accept anybody's idea of what her limitations should be, she set records nobody would ever break.

3

FIRST STEP IN
THE LONGEST JOURNEY
Discovery of Flight, 1917–22

Amelia was always pushing into unknown seas.

Mrs. Sutherland-Brown
Ogontz School for Girls

Christmas 1917. Somehow money was scraped together to send Amelia to the Ogontz School for Girls in Rydal, Pennsylvania. For the holiday, she and her mother visited Muriel in Toronto, where she attended St. Margaret's College. That same year the United States had entered World War I. Canada had been fighting in it for nearly four years and had the wounded as evidence, men who were blind or paralyzed, or without arms or legs. It was in Toronto that Amelia realized what war meant. While she and her mother were walking down King Street, four young men, not much older than Amelia, passed going the opposite way. They were all amputees. One looked at Amelia, and for a moment their eyes met.

She was not the kind of person who would sit back and say, "Somebody do something." Instead when something needed doing, she figured out what *she* could do and then did it. I'm not going back to the States with you, she told her mother. She would stay to help in one of Canada's hospitals. Her mother argued that would mean she couldn't graduate from Ogontz in the spring. Why didn't she return, finish school, then come back? Amelia's answer was that this was where she belonged. "I want to do something useful in the world," she said. And Amy Earhart, knowing her daughter, knowing there was no talking her out of something once her mind was made up, gave way. Amelia stayed in Toronto with Muriel.

"The war," Amelia later wrote, "was the greatest shock that some lives had had to survive. It so completely changed the direction of my own footsteps that the details of those days remain indelible in my memory. There is so much that must be done in a civilized barbarism like war."

Although she could not make a connection with the American Red Cross, Amelia managed to acquire training as a nurse's aide. The Spadina Military Hospital, in a converted college building, hired her. From 7:00 A.M. to 7:00 P.M. She made beds, scrubbed floors, carried trays, rubbed backs, and in general was "Mary Sunshine" to the wounded veterans. It wasn't difficult, she said, "for me whose IQ is low enough for natural cheerfulness." Slighting references to her abilities, especially her intelligence, often surfaced in her conversations and later in her writings.

With her imagination as active as ever, she thought of ways to make life a little easier for the patients. When the men complained about the rice pudding, she spent her own small earnings to buy them ice cream.

Those days in Canada turned her permanently against war. When invited to speak before the Daughters of the American Revolution (DAR) many years later, she warned them that they might not like what she had to say. Nonetheless the women desperately wanted the famous Amelia Earhart to appear before them, and perhaps in their eagerness they could not believe she would say anything offensive. As always, she spoke her mind honestly. The DAR turned quite chilly as she said the organization was in part responsible for wars by not speaking out against them. Women should be drafted along with men, she said. That way the male "glory" found in battle would be greatly lessened, and once that happened, she believed, men would stop hurrying to slaughter one another.

It was also in Toronto that her indifference toward aviation was reversed. "In every life there are places at which the individual, looking back, can see he was forced to choose one of several paths. These turning points may be marked by a trivial circumstance or by one of great joy or sorrow."

In the winter of 1918, a captain in the Royal Flying Corps, a friend she made while horseback riding, invited Amelia Earhart to come watch some flying. There were airfields around Toronto where officers were trained.

Later she was always able to recall the sting of snow hitting her face as it was thrown back from the propellers of those planes taking off on skis. She longed to ride along, but no civilian passengers were allowed.

Despite the hardships and dangers of flying at that time, or perhaps because of them, flying was highly dashing and romantic. Pilots were regarded somewhat like movie stars, with their helmets and goggles, white silk scarves tossed carelessly around their necks and streaming in the wind of the open cockpits. Amelia was fascinated, listening to them joke about the danger. They laughed about greasing their faces to keep them from freezing at high altitudes. They kidded each other about wearing padded helmets, which supposedly would protect their heads in a crash. Planes were flimsy then, underpowered, and motors were unpredictable. So what made men want to fly? Nobody could tell her. Obviously they loved doing it, but why? She wanted to understand that feeling, wanted to try it herself.

Those months in Toronto when she stood in the cold, watching planes take off and land, Amelia Earhart felt a great tug toward aviation. "Perhaps it was the glamour of the environment, the times, or my youth," she said. "Aviation had come close to me. I determined then I would some day ride one of these devil machines."

Way before the pioneering women pilots Harriet Quimby and Blanche Scott took to the skies, women went up in balloons. They were no strangers to the demands of flight. France, being more open-minded about women fliers, saw more than its share of female air pioneers. Madeleine Sophie Blanchard flew a solo balloon in 1805, and became aeronaut to Napoleon. Aida de Acosta, Cuban born, made one of the world's first dirigible flights over Paris.

Still society generally ignored the bravery and accomplishments of these women. During her year and a half at the Ogontz School, Amelia Earhart kept a scrapbook of women's achievements, particularly those of explorers. "Poor relatives in the houses of the mighty," she called them, referring to the fact that they were moving in a so-called man's world.

Mixed in her were paradoxical characteristics. She was practical yet a dreamer, a romantic with a love of poetry yet a realist. Quiet and polite, she held strong ideas. At Ogontz she argued for intellectual freedom, a revolutionary notion for a young woman then. She thought sororities should be democratic. By paying attention to women pathfinders, she saw that in fact women could do almost anything a man could.

Surely she read about Raymonde de Laroche, a leading lady in French society, who decided to learn to fly and became the world's first licensed woman pilot. Perhaps she read that de Laroche believed that some people spread the risks of a lifetime over many years, while others, like herself, pack them into minutes—or hours. "In my case," she said, "what is to happen will happen." This could have been Amelia herself talking, the philosophy of both women was so similar.

De Laroche learned to fly on her 23rd birthday, when she presented herself at the Châlons Airfield. Since this was France and not the United States, and since she had the francs to spend, she was at once put aboard a Voisin, which looked like a box kite. Her instructor told her to proceed at a slow pace along the ground, which she did, as he ran beside the plane. At the end of the field, the plane was lifted around to face the other way. Do the same thing again, the instructor declared, but de Laroche had her own ideas. "I'm ready to fly," she said, and tore off down the airstrip without another word. The Voisin finally lifted off the ground up to about 15 feet, flew a short distance, then bumped back to earth. Of course women like de Laroche would refuse to take a back seat to someone just because he happened to be a man.

Despite evidence to the contrary, most people still held that women, by nature, were unable to withstand the speeds, altitudes, or pressures of flying. Men tried to prove the idea true by tampering with women's flying equipment or emptying gas from the tanks of their airplanes. They said women would "domesticate" flying. This so-called domestication actually proved a plus later when airlines hired women to act as spokespersons to help people overcome their fear of air travel. Amelia was one of the pioneers in this effort as well.

But in Toronto that year of 1918, aviation wasn't even considered a possible career for women. For Amelia Earhart then it was simply something she wanted to try. "She loved adventuring of the spirit and body," wrote her husband, George Putnam. She was never content with things as they were, and always liked to try something new. At the same time, American women were mounting their strongest effort toward getting the vote. These stirrings and the independence many had felt by entering the job force during World War I had an effect on all women's psyche and dreams. Change was coming.

For a woman who wanted to escape the bonds of what society expected, there were only two ways: Become a movie star or go into aviation. It was much easier to get on the silver screen than it was to fly.

Armistice came on November 11, 1918. Before leaving Toronto, Amelia attended the Toronto Exposition with a friend. During aerial acrobatics, a small red plane caught Amelia's attention as it looped and spun and buzzed above. Then it climbed higher, higher, until it turned and headed straight for the ground and the group of people with whom Amelia and her friend were standing. She had seen planes dive before and pull out at the last minute. So Amelia watched the plane, decided the pilot had it under control, and stood her ground while everyone else ran. The plane whined toward her. She admitted later she was frightened but refused to budge. "Common sense told me that if something went wrong with the mechanism or if the pilot lost control, he, the airplane and I would be rolled up in a ball together."

About 50 feet away, close enough for Amelia to see almost every detail of the plane and the pilot's face, close enough for her to feel the noise vibration of the engine in her bones, the pilot pulled up. "I did not understand at the time," she said, "but I believe that little red airplane said something to me as it swished by."

Her practical plans for the future turned to medical school. She decided to become a doctor, having developed in Canada what she called "a yen for medicine." Before returning to the States, she became a patient herself. First came a bout with pneumonia, then a sinus infection that caused pain around one eye and severe headaches. This recurred throughout her life, especially when she was under stress. After several operations to drain her sinuses, she joined her mother and sister in Massachusetts to recuperate. Here she took a class in automobile engine repair. She'd always been a tinkerer, fascinated with mechanical things. Money was scarce, though Amy's trust fund had finally been released to her through the courts.

Once Amelia took part of the grocery money to buy a second-hand banjo, which she taught herself to play. She had an ear for music. Her picking the banjo suggests a more playful Amelia Earhart than the public AE, as she eventually became known.

In the fall of 1919, she began studying premed at Columbia University in New York City. At the same time she took classes in French poetry. When a medical test question stumped her, she would quote a favorite line from a poem.

Meanwhile, Edwin Earhart had stopped drinking, become a Christian Scientist, and, lured by the idea of a new start in the West, moved to California. He set up a law practice there and wrote Amy asking her to join him. He wanted another try at their marriage. Amy pressed Amelia to come along when her school term was done. Hoping she could be of help in patching up her parents' union, Amelia headed for Los Angeles with her mother. After a year or so, she would return to pick up her life again. It was early summer. Amelia was nearly 23.

As Broadway is to actors, California was then to pilots— the place to be. It was a hotbed for aviation. Amelia coaxed her father into going along with her to air circuses, where barnstormers gave rides, and others walked on wings or jumped from planes wearing parachutes. Generally a fear of flying gripped the country with word of crashes and sometimes fatalities connected with flying. Nonetheless curiosity brought huge crowds to airfields. The notion of flying seemed to awaken something basic in people.

At one circus on Daugherty Field near Long Beach, Amelia got her father to make inquiries for her. "Dad, please ask that officer how long it takes to learn to fly."

"The answer to that is a thousand dollars. But why do you want to know?"

As dust rose in clouds from the dirt runway, and the air roared with the noise of airplane engines revving or opened up for takeoff, Amelia Earhart admitted, "I think I'd like to fly."

Assuming she meant a ride, Edwin talked with someone about it and made an appointment for her to go aloft the next day.

Barnstormer pilot Frank Hawks, who later became famous for setting speed records, took Amelia up on her first break with the bonds of earth. The flight took place in a field near Wilshire Boulevard, an open space surrounded by oil wells. Dust from the runway was choking and the sun hot.

The cockpit had two compartments with a set of controls in each. Hawks sat in the back and indicated that his passenger should sit up front. Planes were hard to climb into, and required getting up onto the wing before slithering down into a seat. Another man came along to squeeze in beside Amelia so that he could grab her if she proved to be what men around airfields called "a nervous lady," and tried to jump out. A mechanic swung the propeller to start the engine, then Hawks taxied the plane to the end of the field.

The thrill Amelia felt as Frank Hawks prepared for takeoff must have been a thousand times greater than any experienced today on modern aircraft. Here was something completely new for her, combining the elements she loved: adventure, risk, speed. Hawks turned the plane. She looked out over the nose to see the open runway ahead. She had seen enough takeoffs to know what came next: the surge of speed, the bumping off the ground, and then—disconnection and soaring. Quietly, sitting very still, she waited. Hawks gunned the motor. He rammed the throttle forward to the firewall. Engine wide open, they raced down the runway—then lifted off. It was an historic event—which no one noticed as anything special, except Amelia Earhart, for whom the event meant everything. She knew. She saw. And she loved it.

"Miles away I saw the ocean . . . the Hollywood hills smiled at me over the edge of the cockpit. We were friends, the ocean, the hills, I." Not even 300 feet off the ground, she already knew she must learn to fly.

At one point the stick in front of her angled forward as Hawks maneuvered. Instinctively, she reached out for it. The man beside her shook his head and pushed aside her hand.

That night Amelia told her family casually over dinner, "I think I'd like to learn to fly," knowing well, she said, she would die if she didn't.

Her parents greeted this news just as casually. Knowing they probably didn't take her seriously, she lined up an instructor, then approached them about money.

Edwin was shocked. Surely she was joking. He couldn't afford a thousand dollars for her lessons. Probably he also thought if he didn't pay, she wouldn't fly. Instead she took a clerical job at a phone company to begin to pay for lessons.

Her work there, she said, consisted of filing letters, then trying to find them again. For a while she also took up photography and opened a studio with a friend. When that business collapsed, she took a job with a commercial photographer.

Deciding that she would be less "embarrassed" to have a female teach her to fly, Amelia asked Neta Snook, one of America's first women pilots, if she'd be willing. Neta even agreed to give Amelia lessons on limited credit. Pay as she could.

Neta Snook was the first woman to graduate from the Curtiss School of Aviation. A maverick herself, she didn't worry about appearances and wore coveralls to the field. That combined with her red hair and freckles made her stand out in the crowd. It's easy to understand why Amelia gravitated to her as a teacher and mentor.

To reach the airfield for lessons, Amelia rode for an hour by streetcar to the outskirts of Los Angeles. Then she walked three miles along the highway. Once a woman and her daughter gave her a lift. In the car, Amelia told them she was going to be a pilot. Though excited by that news, the little girl objected, saying Amelia's hair was too long for that, since all the aviatrixes she'd seen pictures of had their hair bobbed.

"In 1920 it was very odd for a woman to fly, and I had tried to remain as normal as possible in looks in order to offset the usual criticism of my behavior." Even so, Amelia had secretly been taking snips at her hair.

The gear she hit on consisted of riding breeches, high leather boots, and a leather jacket she bought for $20 and slept in so it wouldn't look new. Then in the cockpit, like other pilots, she wore a leather helmet and goggles.

During lessons, Amelia sat in back with Neta in front. A duplicate set of controls let her feel the moves as Neta made them. The engines on these small planes made such a noise that people had to shout to be barely heard. Like cars of the times, which were started by being cranked in the front, the engines of these planes were started by a mechanic cranking the propeller.

Before this type of arrangement, students went up in what were called "penguin" planes because they hopped along no more than a few feet off the ground. They required many landings, and takeoffs, good practice for students. Another name for these planes was "grass cutter." However, when time came to solo in an airplane that actually rose high into the air, most students stayed up until their gas was nearly gone out of fear of bringing the plane down to earth, one of the most precise maneuvers a pilot has to make.

"As with most activities," Amelia said, "it's far easier to start something than it is to finish it. Almost every beginner hops off with a whoop of joy, though he is likely to end his flight with something akin to DTs."

In a few lessons, Amelia learned to fly in line with fences around a field, coordinating the stick, the rudder, and the throttle. This gave her the necessary skills for landing the plane. Sitting in back, she watched Neta Snook take the craft through spins and stalls—when the plane loses air speed so it no longer moves forward, thus making it a heavy weight in the sky and in danger of falling.

Once she and Neta rose to about 50 feet when the motor suddenly cut off and they landed in a cabbage patch. AE said, "I bit my tongue." To her the crash was an interesting experience. She could see it coming and it seemed as though minutes passed as they approached the cabbages, although actually it was only a matter of seconds. She reached over to cut the switch before they hit the ground, thus reducing the chances of fire. Even as a student, her head was cool in emergencies.

Anne Morrow Lindbergh, wife of Charles Lindbergh, and a pilot as well as a navigator and poet, was entranced by the "magic" of flying. Amelia Earhart was struck most of all by the beauty. After only two and one half hours of instruction, she decided life would not be complete until she owned her own airplane. Not yet having learned to solo, she wanted to surpass herself.

But how could she buy a plane when she could barely afford flying lessons? Progress was slow, as "my economic status itself remained a bit in the air," she said. During this time, the Earharts took in boarders to make their own ends meet. One was Sam Chapman, a chemical engineering graduate of Tufts University and a New Englander. He became Amelia Earhart's first serious boyfriend. Their idea of an evening out was to attend political meetings, not unlike Amelia's mother, Amy, when she was a young woman of similar age.

Muriel came to California during the summer and accompanied Amelia to the airfield. They brought along a picnic lunch that Amy had packed. Cheerfully Muriel helped repair and shellack the fabric wings of airplanes at the field. Amelia told her, "It's so breathtaking up there, I want to fly whenever I can."

Neta Snook ran out of money and had to sell her airplane. Forced to look around for a replacement instructor, Amelia approached John Montijo, a former Army trainer and a fine pilot. "I want to learn stunting," she told him, because she wanted to be prepared for any emergency in the air.

Neta Snook and Muriel watched from the ground the day Amelia soloed. She had had approximately 10 hours of instruction. Her hair by then was quite short and would never grow long again. She wore her leather jacket and high boots. Calmly she taxied the airplane to the end of the runway, turned, revved the engines, then the plane leaped forward. Suddenly the right wing sagged. "The mental agony of starting the plane had just been gone through," she said, "and I was suddenly faced with the agony of stopping it."

She cut the throttle, pulled back the spark control lever, and the plane settled reluctantly. A shock absorber had broken, she learned at the hangar. Repairs were made, and she again attempted to take off. This time she made it, climbing, turning, and at last pranking in the sky. On her own at 5,000 feet, seeming not at all nervous, it was as though her heart had taken flight. Finally, and confidently, she circled into a landing pattern. Down she came—but too fast. Nearing the ground, the plane bounced on and off it. After several jolts, she realized she hadn't cut back on the gas, so she pulled the throttle all the way back, held the stick hard, and the plane thumped to the ground in what she called "a thoroughly rotten landing."

"All landings are good ones if you can walk away from them," Montijo simply said.

An Iowa tourist who happened to be at the field snapped Amelia's picture as she climbed from the plane, no doubt to show the folks at home what wild things were happening in California.

Free now to go off alone in a plane so small that one person could pull it around the runway by its tail, Amelia Earhart took to the skies as though born to them. Men at the airport grudgingly admitted she was a "natural."

Buying her own plane was the next step. She located a second-hand yellow sports plane, a Kinner Canary, that everyone warned her against buying since such planes were still in the experimental stages. It was the only model the builder had, and if she'd be willing to demonstrate it to poten-

tial buyers of other Kinner models, he would let her have free
hangar space. Actually a sports plane was just what she
wanted, something that "hopped off like a sandpiper and
actually seemed to like it." Most planes, larger, though underpowered, lumbered in takeoff, but not this Kinner. The price
was $2,000.

Aviation demanded great sacrifices from its devotees then,
and Amelia Earhart was willing to pay all its prices in order to
fly.

She bought the Kinner Canary on her 24th birthday, taking
a job driving a sand and gravel truck to augment her income in
order to pay for it. Amy protested that Amelia was never
home, and volunteered to contribute toward the cost of the
plane if she would quit one of her jobs. Amelia agreed. Muriel
also chipped in on the purchase, and the plane was secured.

Happily she explored the skies, becoming a bright yellow
dot that flew out of sight, then reappeared later. Relatives
thought her flying distinctly strange and in general, like many
people, held that flying was an altogether impractical way to
get places. Nonetheless Amy supported and backed Amelia in
this undertaking, knowing that when Amelia wanted to do
something, she would do it no matter what anyone thought,
and all she, as a mother could do, was back her up with love.

Twice Amelia crashed in the Canary. This must have given
her parents some bad moments. Once she landed in mud. The
plane flopped over forward and she hung upside down by her
safety belt. Another time she hit weeds and the plane flipped
again. This time the safety belt snapped and she flew out of the
cockpit but was not injured. She regarded these incidents as
the "flat tires" of flying, and they were not uncommon to
pilots of that era. They didn't stop Amelia Earhart.

Flying in the early 1920's was done in daytime since there
were no instruments for blind flying, and what instruments
were in the planes rarely worked reliably. Pilots flew by
landmarks sighted below, often buzzing down to within 50
feet or so to look around for them. The one hazard then was
telephone wires. The government ran an airmail service that
put some World War I veterans to work. Also, in the mid-
1920's, a young Charles A. Lindbergh flew the St. Louis-to-

Chicago mail route. Mail flying was known as the suicide club. Cockpits were open and the cold at high altitudes could impair judgement. Many pilots carried along bottles of liquor to keep off the cold (or so they said); the liquor of course also deadened their already numbed brains. This could have contributed much to the "club's" disastrous reputation. Lindbergh was about the only pilot of that crew who was not known for drinking.

Passenger travel first made its appearance in the early 1920's, too, as a highly ambitious venture that many sound businessmen thought would never make money. Frequent landings were made for refueling and refreshments. Still there was no night flying. And a passenger could be dumped anywhere if the pilot needed his space for mail.

Preferring privacy, Amelia did not invite anyone along when she took to the skies. She was also reluctant to do public flying, not wanting to be regarded as a female "freak." At first she wouldn't enter air races for the same reason, besides the fact that promoters wanted a man to fly her plane most of the way, then have her take over and claim she'd flown the entire route. (They found it impossible to believe she might be able to do the whole thing alone.) But when there were records within her capacity to challenge, she could not hold back.

Muriel and her father came to an air show in October 1922, and while they waited on the ground, not knowing what she was up to, Amelia took off, her barograph sealed for recording altitude. Climbing higher and higher, pushing the small Canary to its limits, she reached 13,000 feet. She kept climbing.

"I thought the engine would jump out of its frame," she recalled.

Then the engine stalled. The plane turned to dead weight. She spiraled downward. The motor revived at a low altitude. That day she set a woman's altitude record of 14,000 feet on a 60-horsepower engine, about equivalent to that contained in an ordinary motorcycle today. Men had flown higher than that but in more powerful planes.

Unfortunately there is no record of her father and sister's reactions to the news.

Another day Amelia tried to break her own record. Weather was sunny, but a heavy cloud layer engulfed her as she climbed. Sleet pelted the small yellow plane. Fog wiped out all visibility. Snow plastered her goggles. With no instruments to guide her, she decided she'd better get out of "the soup" fast, and dove. Heading toward the ground at high speed, she plummeted from 12,000 to 3,000 feet before she hit clear skies, and pulled up.

Pilots watching criticized her judgment. "What if the fog had gone all the way to the ground?" one asked, because if it had, without instruments to tell her where she was, she would have just kept on going. "We'd have to dig you out in pieces," he said.

"Yes, I suppose you would," was her reply.

Said French pilot Helen Boucher, "Flying is the only profession where courage pays off."

The daring, the courage, the willingness to risk that mark a hero were there in Amelia Earhart from the start.

4

ACROSS THE ATLANTIC
Flight of *The Friendship*, 1928

> Obviously I realized there was a
> measure of danger. Obviously I
> faced the possibility of not returning
> when first I considered going. Once
> faced and settled there really wasn't
> any good reason to refer to it again.
> Amelia Earhart

After World War I airplane design developed at a rapid pace. Each year planes became sturdier and faster than before. This made long-distance flying possible—not always safe or predictable, but possible. Planes were still underpowered, temperamental, and given to engine failure.

The Atlantic Ocean posed the biggest challenge for aviators. Charles A. Lindbergh became an instant hero when he crossed it solo on May 21, 1927. At that time, women thought more modestly. Each wished to be the first to fly over the ocean simply as a passenger.

The reason was they lacked the training given men by the military. Also, they, like Amelia Earhart, were hampered by the enormous expense connected with flying. Women struggled to reach the point where they could even *think* of crossing the Atlantic, since acquiring the skills and the equipment was in itself a giant hurdle.

The attitudes of society were such that women doubted themselves as well. It was the rare person who managed to forge ahead in the world of aviation if she happened to be born female.

Nonetheless, women were losing their lives in an attempt to set records. Princess Anne Lowenstein-Wertheim, age 63, was the first to attempt an aerial crossing as a passenger. It was 1927. She sat in the wicker passenger seat of a single-engine airplane heading for Canada from England with a pilot and copilot. Sighted once over the North Atlantic, they were not seen again.

In the United States, Ruth Elder and Frances Grayson made, in separate incidents, headlines in 1927. Elder, a student pilot, dreamed of crossing the Atlantic but with her flight instructor doing most of the flying. Probably spurred by Lindbergh's success in May, they took off on October 11 but had to ditch northeast of the Azores and were picked up by a passing freighter.

Not so lucky, Frances Grayson refused to accept the fact that planes couldn't withstand those awesome North Atlantic winter storms. She started out from Maine three times that winter and had to turn back each time. Then on December 23 she once more struck out for Newfoundland en route to Europe and vanished on the way.

The toll mounted. In 1927 alone the Atlantic claimed 19 fliers. The following year, undaunted, Elsie Mackay, an English woman, hired a respected war pilot to fly her from England to Canada. On March 28 they took off and also disappeared.

That same spring Mrs. Frederick Guest, wife of the British secretary of state for air in Lloyd George's cabinet, bought a trimotored Fokker aircraft from Commander Richard E. Byrd. Renaming the plane *The Friendship*, she hired Wilmer Stultz to fly her across the Atlantic, and they began to lay plans for the trip.

Also in the spring of 1928, Captain Hilton H. Railey, a retired army captain and head of a public relations firm promoting such notable adventurers as Commander Byrd, stopped into the offices of Putnam's Sons Publishers in New York City to chat with his friend, George Palmer Putnam, whom Amelia had not yet met.

Putnam mentioned he'd heard something about "a wealthy woman" (Mrs. Guest) buying an airplane in order to cross the ocean. Railey hadn't heard about it. They knew of an American woman, Mabel Boll, who was gearing up, but who was the other woman? Flights were sometimes kept secret to bar competitors who might come forward if they heard the news.

To undertake an Atlantic crossing, however, required weeks of preparations. That gave Railey and Putnam time to inquire about the other woman.

"Why don't you find out if you can," Putnam suggested. "See who's involved." The two of them might "crash the gate," he said, "cash in on the stunt." From what Putnam heard, pontoons were being attached to the plane in East Boston, changing it from a land craft to one that could land on water. The pilot would be 27-year-old Wilmer L. "Bill" Stultz.

Stultz was short, blond, and blue-eyed. He had served with the U.S. 634th Aero Squadron in World War I. Then he joined the Navy and flew until 1922. After that, he flew for the Gates Flying Circus. A pilot, navigator, and radio operator well known for his skill, Stultz was also a heavy drinker.

Stultz had told Railey in Boston that he didn't know the identity of the "mystery woman." The only thing he knew was her lawyer's name—David T. Layman.

On calling Layman, Railey learned that the woman who would ride with Stultz was the former Amy Phipps of Pittsburgh, now Mrs. Frederick Guest of New York and London.

It seemed Mrs. Guest's family wasn't happy about her making this trip, having well-founded fears for her safety. In fact, shortly before Railey placed his call to Mr. Layman, she had given in to the family's wishes and agreed not to make the trip on one condition—that an American girl "of the right image" be found to take her place. So the flight was still going to be made, and the search for this special woman was on.

Grayson suggested that perhaps Railey and Putnam could be of help in finding such a person. Eager to be part of the prospect, the men agreed.

Meanwhile fate had conspired to bring Amelia to Boston. Her parents' 29-year marriage had ended for good, and when her mother offered to pay expenses, Amelia agreed to drive across country to join up with Muriel, who had been teaching school in Medford, Massachusetts (close to Boston), for several years.

Amy and Amelia headed north first in order to see national parks along the way.

"Aren't we going East at all?" Amy asked finally.

"Not until we reach Seattle," was her daughter's jaunty reply. She wanted to see everything.

By the time they hit Boston, the Kissel touring car, which Amelia had bought from the sale of her Canary, was full of tourist stickers, so she could barely see through the windshield. The cheery yellow car, with wire wheels and a convertible top, was probably a "bit outspoken" for Boston, although it had been perfect at home in California.

And in California, Sam Chapman played a waiting game. He took it as a good omen that Amelia was preparing to settle down when she sold her plane in order to buy a car. He believed that one day she would give up her playful hobby and marry him. The only problem in the way: She refused to accept that a woman belonged in the home.

Medical research, that's what she would study, she decided, and took some courses. Then Amy's inheritance was gone, and reaching the age of 28, Amelia decided she'd better get a steady job, some security. Muriel was teaching, so she would, too.

The Extension Department of the University of Massachusetts hired her to teach English. Later she also applied at Denison House in Boston for the job of English teacher to immigrant children from Italy, China, Syria, and Greece.

Marian Perkins, head of Denison, saw before her a young woman who was an unusual mixture of the practical and the artistic, and responded by giving Amelia the position. It was 1926 when she took the job on Tyler Street for $60 a month and began teaching youngsters not just English but a whole philosophy of life. Fresh experiences teach you and keep you young, she told them, and the echoes of Grandfather Otis' teaching came through clearly. She said that meeting new people and encountering new situations make life an interesting adventure. Sometimes she took the children for rides in her roadster, and she tried to instill in them an enthusiasm for life that she believed would help them escape from their bonds of poverty.

All the while she kept dabbling in flying.

On weekends she flew. She demonstrated a Kinner plane to prospective buyers occasionally, and she judged a model airplane tournament for "sheer fun." Amelia joined a local chapter of the National Aeronautical Association, eventually becoming its first woman V.P.

Sam Chapman moved to Boston in hopes of coaxing her into marrying him, while mother Amy encouraged her daughter to follow her heart. Her heart led her to the airfield.

She wrote pilot Ruth Nichols, whom she had never met but had heard about, "I'm a social worker who flies for sport," and asked if Nichols would be interested in organizing a group of women flyers. "I do not claim to be a feminist but do rather enjoy seeing women tackling all kinds of new problems—new for them that is."

By 1928 it was possible to fly across the country in 32 hours. Planes carried up to four passengers, sometimes even in enclosed cabins. The potential for aviation was expanding rapidly.

While she was yet an unknown flier at Denison House, Amelia Earhart wrote a poem she showed to Marian Perkins. It was titled: "The Soul's Dominion."

> Courage is the price that life exacts for granting
>   peace.
> The soul that knows it not knows no release
> From little things:
> Knows not the livid loneliness of fear
> Nor mountain heights where bitter joy can hear
> The sound of wings.
>
> How can life grant us boon of living, compensate
> For dull gray ugliness and pregnant hate

Unless we dare
The soul's dominion? Each time we make a choice
   we pay
With courage to behold resistless day
And grant it fair.

Soon she would have a chance to put this philosophy to the test.

In asking about a suitable female passenger for *The Friendship* trip, Captain Railey went to Rear Admiral Reginald Belknap, among others. Belknap, who had heart of Amelia's flying activities in Boston, thought a moment, then said yes; he knew of a young social worker who flew. "Call Denison House," he told Railey, "and ask for Amelia Earhart."

April 19, 1928. "The opportunity came as casually as an invitation to a matinee; and it came by telephone," said Amelia. It was afternoon. Amelia was teaching and living at Denison. You're wanted on the telephone, someone told her. She said she was busy. Ask the party to call back later. Another message came: He says it's important. Alright, she would take the call.

"Hello. You don't know me but my name is Railey—Captain Hilton Railey. Would you be willing to do something important for the cause of aviation?"

At first she thought this was a joke. She asked for Railey's references before he could ask for hers. And good ones they were, too, she admitted later. That night she went to see Railey, bringing Marian Perkins along just in case the man was not what he said he was.

What struck Railey about her was something she could not have predicted, and that was her uncanny resemblance to Charles A. Lindbergh—Lucky Lindy. Like him, she was confident but shy. She would not become a prima donna. Hiding his excitement, Railey told her a bit about the flight, then arranged for her to go to New York to be interviewed by the "selection committee," composed of George Putnam, David Layman, the lawyer, and John Phipps, Mrs. Guest's brother.

She tried, in that interview, to be charming enough so the "gentlemen" would want to send her, yet not so charming that they would be loathe to let her risk her life. What flying experience did she have, they wanted to know. In the event of a disaster, would she absolve them of all responsibility? What would she do when the flight was over?

As for her, she had some questions of her own. Would she get to do some flying herself? The idea of going along as an "extra weight" did not appeal to her.

She was to receive no pay, no rewards. (Pilot Stultz would receive $20,000. Lou Gordon, mechanic and navigator, would get $5,000.) Even worse, if Amelia earned any money afterward on newspaper articles based on the trip, she would have to turn that money over to the sponsor.

The committee was also struck by her resemblance to Lindbergh in both personality and appearance. George Putnam took her to the train. If she was chosen, he'd be in touch.

For two days she waited, not knowing if the flight was on or if someone else had been chosen for it. If asked, of course she would go. "Who could refuse such a shining adventure?" she said. It would not be done for fame, certainly not for money. She would fly *The Friendship*, if asked, because she loved flying as much as she loved new experiences, because she loved to travel, and because she felt most alive when taking risks.

The call came. They wanted her on this trip. Everything must be kept secret to avoid having potential competitors turn it into a race. There must be no hurry in the preparations that might endanger the lives of the crew.

Amelia told neither her mother nor her sister about the flight, which would be the greatest adventure of her life so far. While the Fokker continued to be modified and outfitted, she kept teaching at Denison House, but in her free time she moved in a new and heady circle of the rich, the famous, the explorers of her time.

Seats were removed and extra fuel tanks installed in the airplane. There would be no place for her to sit at the chart table behind the tanks, just room enough to squat on a rolled-up flying suit, look out the window, and write notes in the logbook. The latest radio equipment was installed, allowing them to contact ships at sea for confirmation of their heading.

She asked Sam Chapman to break the news to Muriel and her mother after she had taken off. "I couldn't stand the added strain," Amelia told Muriel later, "of telling mother and you."

Finally the ship was ready, but the weather was bad. In New York, U.S. Weather Bureau meteorologist Dr. James H. Kimball worked with all the aviators to predict weather patterns to help them decide when to push off and when to hold back. Reports from England were cabled to him daily, as was information from oceangoing vessels. Rain and fog plagued the East Coast that May.

Waiting out the weather, the crew, along with George Putnam and Captain Railey, often went to dinner and the theater. Eva Le Gallienne played in *The Good Hope* that spring in Boston. A recurring line in the show, "The fish are dearly paid for," became a motto for *The Friendship* group.

Stultz started drinking heavily. He was 27. Lou Gordon, the mechanic, was 26. Amelia Earhart was one month away from her 31st birthday. At that time she had put in a few hundred hours in small planes whenever she could afford it. Nonetheless, hers was the first license granted an American woman by the Fédération Aéronautique Internationale. She was not trained in instrument flying, nor had she flown a craft with three engines. Still she hoped to take the controls sometime during the flight.

For three weeks the plane sat ready to go. When weather was clear in the mid–Atlantic, it was foggy in Boston. There was either too little wind, too much fog, or excessively high waves. Seas and weather both had to be perfect for a water takeoff.

On two separate days, the crew with alternate pilot Lou Gower rode the tug *Sadie Ross* to where *The Friendship* lay at anchor in East Boston harbor. "The ship's golden wings with their spread of 72 feet were strong and exquisitely fashioned," Amelia wrote. They tried on both days but couldn't get off the water.

Then early on June 3, a windy Sunday morning, the four tried again. Stultz started the engines. Lou Gordon unhitched the anchor lines. The plane swung out into the harbor, turned, and skimmed the surface. Nothing happened. Stultz slowed and taxied back into position. Again they tried but could not get off the water. The *Sadie Ross* was signaled. Lou Gower left the plane in order to lighten the load. With 900 gallons of gasoline aboard, it was heavy and unwieldy. The tug trailed the red and gold plane as Stultz once more shoved the throttle to the firewall. From where she sat next to a can of water, Amelia Earhart watched the air speed indicator. The needle rose, 45–50–60, and they were bound for Nova Scotia at 6:30 A.M., June 3, 1928. From Nova Scotia, after refueling, they would take off across the Atlantic.

Wearing brown riding pants, a brown leather jacket, brown sweater, white silk blouse, and a colorful scarf, Amelia jotted notes in the log as they climbed, making a wide northeast arc in the sky. Suddenly the cabin door flew open. Amelia lunged for it, holding it shut while Gordon climbed back from the cockpit to secure it with a rope to a heavy gasoline can. He returned to the front. The can came sliding across the floor. Yelling for Gordon, Amelia jumped for the rope. The Atlantic Ocean yawned 2,000 feet below as the door swung out pulling gas can and Amelia Earhart in its wake. Rolling within inches of the door, she held on while Gordon struggled to close it. Finally the door was tied shut, and the flight continued more calmly.

Two hours passed in haze and wind. The cabin was cold. Briefly they landed in Halifax, Nova Scotia. After three hours they took off for Newfoundland. Thick fog forced them to return to Halifax.

Meanwhile George Putnam in Boston notified the press that a woman was on her way to Newfoundland aboard an airplane called *The Friendship* in an attempt to be the first of her sex to fly across the Atlantic. Reporters hounded the crew at the Dartmouth Hotel, making it hard to sleep. Amelia was disturbed by the stories they "made up about us all."

Morning, 9:45. They took off again. Sighting a steamer below, Amelia wrote, "I wonder if she knows who we are. I wonder if we know."

In Medford, before Sam Chapman had a chance to break the news to Amelia's sister and mother, a reporter came to the house and peppered Mrs. Earhart with questions. By now her hearing was very poor, and, too, she was not used to being asked intimate questions by strangers. "What do you think of your daughter flying the Atlantic?" the reporter asked. "I think she's too smart to try," said Amy tartly. And then she found out that this is exactly what Amelia was planning to do.

At 12:50 P.M., June 4, they spotted Newfoundland; at 2:50 St. Mary's Bay; and at 3:00 they set down in Trepassy Bay, Newfoundland, and were instantly surrounded by small boats. Gordon climbed onto a pontoon to wave away the boats and was nearly knocked into the water by a friendly throw of a tow line.

While they hoped to gas up and move on quickly, Stultz, Gordon, and Earhart ended up staying at Devereux House in Newfoundland for 13 days as the wind blew and the fog rolled in. Even gas could not be loaded aboard in the bad weather. Meanwhile newspapers in the States ran front-page stories on this unknown named Amelia Earhart. They said she was making the dangerous trip in order to restore a lost family fortune. **GIRL PILOT DARES THE ATLANTIC**, read one newspaper headline. From Newfoundland, Amelia cabled her family.

KNOW YOU WILL UNDERSTAND WHY I COULD NOT TELL PLANS OF FLIGHT STOP DON'T WORRY STOP NO MATTER WHAT HAPPENS IT WILL HAVE BEEN WORTH THE TRYING STOP LOVE AMELIA

Her mother valiantly cabled back:

WE ARE NOT WORRYING STOP WISH I WERE WITH YOU STOP GOOD LUCK AND CHEERIO STOP LOVE MOTHER

Between rummy games with Lou Gordon, while Stultz drank, Amelia walked the beach and read the cables that poured in. Sometime during the long wait, Stultz got into the plane and taxied wildly about the harbor nearly colliding with moored fishing boats and the rocky breakwater.

Their nerves stretched taut as the wait went on. Still no go-ahead from Doc Kimball in New York.

Lou Gordon finally wanted to give up the venture and return to Boston. Amelia convinced him to hang on for just a few more days. She told no one about what was happening. If she complained, they might think she was getting cold feet. She did not want people thinking she was an hysterical female. So she stayed quiet and kept her eye on Stultz and his drinking, recognizing in his behavior much that was sickeningly familiar from years past with her father.

Toward the end of the waiting, even she almost gave up on Stultz. All she had to do was cable George Putnam and have Lou Gower sent; still she said nothing. Surely Stultz would snap out of his stupor once they got the go-ahead. Knowing only that the long wait was frustrating, George Putnam cabled Amelia: SUGGEST YOU TURN IN AND HAVE YOUR LAUNDRY DONE.

If he didn't know the kind of person he was dealing with before, he learned with her response: THANKS FATHERLY TELEGRAM STOP NO WASHING NECESSARY STOP SOCKS UNDERWEAR WORN OUT STOP SHIRT LOST TO SLIM [Lou Gordon] AT RUMMY STOP CHEERIO AE. As though a new person had metamorphosed out of the first, from there on she was known as AE, and that's how she preferred it.

They ate canned rabbit and canned fish and even the eggs tasted fishy because the hens in Newfoundland lived on a diet of fish. Lou Gordon got by on candy bars from the local store. When *The Friendship* left, the candy shelves were bare.

Not far from anyone's thoughts was Mabel Boll, who had tried to hire Stultz away from *The Friendship*. He had wavered but then stuck with his original commitment. Nonetheless, Boll had assembed another crew and flown her single-engine plane *Columbia* to Harbor Grace, Newfoundland. At the same time as Amelia waited poised for takeoff from Trepassy Bay, Boll also waited to get into the skies. With Mabel Boll breathing down their backs, the crew wanted to get into the air as quickly as possible. The wait became intolerable.

They waited so long that people stopped showing up every day to see if they would fly. When conditions were finally right, there was nobody on hand to see them go, except Pops from the local store.

It was June 17, 11:00 A.M. AE and Gordon struggled with Stultz, half carrying him to the water. Once involved in the flight, they hoped he would sober up. It was impossible to tell at that point whether he would or not.

To lighten the load for takeoff, they removed 200 of the 900 gallons of gasoline, an inflatable rubber life raft, and life preservers. That meant there was no margin for error. Everything had to work perfectly.

They needed wind from the southeast for takeoff out of the narrow harbor. Kimball's report cabled by George Putnam predicted fair weather over the Grand Banks and North Atlantic for the next 48 hours. Three times Stultz taxied, attempted a takeoff, only to cut speed as they reached the open ocean. "Just try once more," AE urged. On the fourth try, engine sputtering from salt spray, the airplane lifted off the water and headed for England. ("Pops," back in Newfoundland, waited a half hour, according to AE's instructions, then sent a one-word code cable to George Putnam: VIOLET.) They were on their way.

From where she sat, AE watched the tight muscles in Stultz's face ease with time. She noted weather and air speed in the log. By noon Stultz seemed more rational, his eyes were clearer. Fog swallowed up the plane.

Amelia found a bottle of brandy stowed, and thought of tossing it overboard. Then she decided that if they ran into trouble, and Bill Stultz needed his brandy as a crutch, it might be better to have it on hand, and she put the bottle back where she found it.

Flying in fog is like having a black cloth over your eyes, AE described later in one of her books. This meant relying on the precision of instruments that were in their most rudimentary stage of development. They hit pelting rains and winds that knocked about the plane worse than AE had ever experienced. Rain became a snowstorm and the plane shook violently in turbulent drafts of air.

Seeing clouds towering ahead, Stultz upended the plane and dove without warning. Amelia tumbled against the chart table, clinging to it to keep from falling over the gas tanks. Finding no break in the cloud cover, Stultz reversed direction by climbing. "Jazzing," AE called it. They went from 1,000 to 5,000 feet. In the logbook she compared cloud formations to mountains and icebergs, and said, "I am getting housemaid's knee kneeling here at the table gulping beauty."

In the States, George Putnam held letters to give to her family in the event of her death. "Popping off letters" she called them.

To her father:

> Dearest Dad:
> Hooray for the last grand adventure! I wish I had won but it was worthwhile anyway . . .

To her mother:

> Even though I have lost, the adventure was worth the while. Our family tends to be too secure. My life has been really very happy. And I don't mind contemplating its end in the midst of it.

To Muriel:

> Dear Scrappy:
> I have tried to play for a large stake and if I succeed all will be well. If I don't, I shall be happy to pop off in the midst of such an adventure . . .

8:00 P.M. "I think I am happy," she wrote in the log. "Sad admission of scant intellectual equipment."

Then, "Strong head winds. Wonderful time. Bill says the radio is cuckoo." With the radio out, they could not get directions from ships at sea.

Darkness came at 10:00 P.M. "Darkness complete. There are many hours to go." The only light came from the instrument panel and the occasional flash of Lou Gordon's flashlight on the compass. They proceeded on the basis of dead reckoning. There was the constant worry that they might be off course and have no way of knowing it. The temperature dropped in the cabin. AE put on the furlined flying suit she had borrowed from a friend in Boston who didn't know why she needed it.

At 3:30 A.M. dawn came. There was nothing to see but fog. "Sounds as if all motors are cutting. Bill opens her wide to clear her . . . fog awful."

AE wrote nothing of beauty then. The tension of that dawn is clear in what she didn't write.

6:15 A.M. They should have spotted Ireland but saw nothing. They had been aloft 16 hours and had four to five hours of fuel left. At 6:30 they spotted a ship, the luxury ocean liner *America*. But instead of paralleling their course as they thought it should be, the ship was cutting across it. Were they lost? Stultz circled, hoping the ship's captain would see their plane and paint bearings on the deck, as some ships did then to help out planes. No sailors scurried to paint anything below them, so AE wrote a note, wrapped it around an orange, opened the hatch and dropped it. The orange fell. It missed. Hurriedly she wrote again, wrapped a second message, sent it hurtling, and missed again. Should they land hear the ship? They would not get up again on those choppy seas, Stultz pointed out. Or should they keep on flying?

As they debated, a conversation took place on the bridge of the *America*.

"Looks like a reconnaissance plane."

"It can't be one of ours," the captain said. "They're certainly taking a lot of interest in us."

"My God," the first officer shouted. "We're being bombarded!" They watched as the plane stopped circling and continued eastward.

"We all favored sticking to the course," AE said later. "With faith lost in that, it was hopeless to carry on. When last we checked it, before the radio went dead, the plane had been holding true."

With less than two hours of gas left, they plowed on into rain and fog again. "Mess," AE wrote. Gordon pulled out a scrambled egg sandwich and began to eat.

Sighting fishing boats below, Stultz dove so low he almost skimmed the water. They, too, cut across *The Friendship*'s course. What they did not know then was that they had already passed over Ireland in the fog, and these boats were proceeding through the Irish Sea.

They held to their original course all the same. They had been spotting cloud formations for some time, thinking them to be land, so when they sighted the blue line that did not vanish in the sun's rays, they didn't dare hope that this time they were seeing land. They watched as the line grew.

"LAND!" Gordon threw aside his sandwich. Edging up on it, they saw a large mass but had no idea where they were. Stultz followed the shoreline looking for an inlet long enough to take the three-engine Fokker. Twenty hours and 40 minutes after leaving Trepassy, Newfoundland, a weary Bill Stultz brought down the plane into a tidal river. They were half a mile from shore. Gordon climbed out to secure the plane to a buoy. They had landed.

In the rain, a small crowd gathered on the shore. Nobody stirred toward a boat. Irritated, AE said, "I'll get someone to send a boat," and waved her scarf out the window. A man on shore took off his coat and waved it back playfully. After a long while, several boats did venture out, took back the news, but it was two hours before a police launch arrived to take them aboard. It was then they discovered that they had come down at Burry Port, Wales.

Amelia Earhart was the center of attention. People reached out to touch her. Someone stole her scarf. Like astronauts would be returning from the stratosphere, they were mobbed once people found out who they were and what they had done. They were taken through the crowd to Fricker's Metal Company factory, where the foreman's wife fixed them tea. It was 10:00 that night before they managed to have supper, and during all that time, Amelia repeatedly had to stick her head out the window in response to cheers.

This was her first taste of the fame that engulfed her and would not relent from then on. "Amelia never liked publicity," her mother said of her.

From England, Captain Railey, who had sailed there earlier to guide the crew through the hoopla once they landed, sent telegrams for Amelia to her mother and to Marian Perkins. They simply said, "LOVE AMELIA."

It had been an all-night wait for Amy and Muriel. "Well now that it's over I'll have a chance to catch up on my mending," Amy said, and went off to bed. Muriel was in a state of near collapse.

This was the first aerial crossing of the Atlantic by a woman, and the first by a seaplane.

Burry Port later erected an 18-foot monument to the *Friendship* mission, to Amelia Earhart, Wilmer Stultz, and Lou Gordon.

But when Railey arrived to guide the crew through the enormous celebrations awaiting them, he found one frustrated hero.

"It was a grand experience," she told him, "but all I did was lie on my tummy and take pictures of the clouds. I was just baggage like a sack of potatoes."

"What of it? You're still the first woman to fly the Atlantic, and what's more the first woman pilot."

"Oh well," she was unmoved by his argument, "maybe some day I'll try it alone."

5

NO BLUSHING BRIDE
Marriage to George Putnam, 1928-1932

> It is through what we care about that
> we grow into what we were meant to
> be.
>
> Merle Shain
> *Hearts That We Broke Long Ago*

T ugs and steamer horns blasted as *The Friendship* touched down in the water off Southampton, England. Throngs cheered on the docks and on the streets. The quiet, serious young woman from Atchison, Kansas, was shocked by her instant fame. The spotlight was on her. Every move she made, every thing she wore, every word she said was examined, reported, discussed, applauded. In many ways this struck her as ridiculous, and not a little annoying. "The accident of sex made me chief performer in our particular sideshow," she said. All the cheering only made her realize more deeply what a poor opinion most people had of women, that they would get so excited at her ability simply to ride in an airplane.

She tried to shift credit to Stultz and Gordon, to the manufacturers of the Fokker, to the trip's sponsors, to Mrs. Guest. The crowds only wanted to see her, touch her. They took her response as humility and were all the more charmed by her. The more she tried to evade praise, the more it was heaped on her. Nobody was interested in the two men from the trip.

Captain Railey said, "Whether laying a wreath at the Cenotaph or before a statue of Edith Cavell, whether sipping tea with the Prime Minister . . . or talking with Winston Churchill, she remained herself, serious, forthright . . ."

She was taken from the harbor to London in a yellow Rolls Royce. (The color yellow was one of her favorites, though she never wore it, and it seems to appear regularly at stages in her life.) There she stayed with Mrs. Guest on Park Lane.

A cable of congratulations came from President Calvin Coolidge. Amelia cabled back:

SUCCESS ENTIRELY DUE GREAT SKILL OF MR. STULTZ STOP HE WAS ONLY ONE MILE OFF

Reception in England after Friendship *flight, 1928*

COURSE AT VALENTIA AFTER FLYING BLIND FOR
TWO THOUSAND TWO HUNDRED FORTY SIX
MILES AT AVERAGE SPEED ONE HUNDRED AND
THIRTEEN MPH.

Though she desperately wanted a future in aviation, she
would not bargain for it by taking undeserved praise.

Still there was some criticism in the background. The
Church Times of London wrote: "The voyage itself for nearly
all the way through fog is a remarkable achievement made
possible by the skill and courage of the pilot. But his anxiety
must have been vastly increased by the fact that he was carrying a woman passenger." Another reporter pointed out that
she owed her fame to someone else's skill. Her fairy-tale
success no doubt made some people jealous, and men who
thought women belonged on the ground could be counted on
to find excuses for a feminine success.

Amelia Earhart was not one to fool herself. In fact, she
leaned far in the opposite direction, taking little note of the
courage it took for her to make the *Friendship* flight. "I'm a
false heroine," she told Railey. "Some day I'll redeem my self-
respect. I can't live without it."

She was swept up into parties, teas, testimonial dinners, ex-
hibits, with Railey as her escort. To refuse to participate
would break her bargain with the trip's committee. To go
along with the fuss made her feel like a fraud.

One night at an American embassy party, word was
brought to her that the Prince of Wales would like the
privilege of a dance. Even in her imaginary trips in the Kansas
buggy, such an invitation would probably have seemed too
farfetched to even pretend, a Kansas girl dancing with a real
prince. It turned out that the prince (who later gave up his
throne to marry the woman he loved) was an amateur aviator
himself, and they danced and danced.

When the parties and ceremonies wound to a close, *The
Friendship* crew boarded the SS *Roosevelt* for home. Stultz
brought a case of brandy along and stayed drunk for most of
the trip. To escape the curiosity of other passengers, Amelia
spent much of her time on the bridge with Captain Harry

Manning. He explained the basics of celestial navigation to her. It was on that voyage that they vowed to one day make a flight together. Nine years later, that vow came true.

On board the *Roosevelt* was a gift that AE somehow got enough money to buy herself while she was in London: The Avro Avian Moth airplane that Lady Mary Heath had flown on her historic solo flight from Capetown, South Africa, to London with a Bible, a shotgun, tennis rackets, tea gowns, and a fur coat aboard.

In New York, George Palmer Putnam waited with invitations from all over the country. His office had been besieged by people wanting, not the male members of *The Friendship* crew, but Amelia Earhart to endorse products, speak at meetings, take jobs. Some wanted her to star in their next movie projects.

Putnam advised Amelia on what to accept and what to turn down: no movies, and only three cities for ticker-tape parades—Boston, Chicago, and New York.

Mayor Jimmy Walker led the New York parade of open cars up Broadway as paper scraps and ticker-tape plumes created a blizzard in the early summer air. In Chicago, Stultz vanished before the parade began, so George Putnam put on a flight suit and goggles and rode in the pilot's place. Nobody noticed the difference. It was Amelia Earhart everyone came to see, and it was, despite her discomfort with being a celebrity, her show all the way.

"Nothing to make a fuss over," she constantly insisted, but nobody listened. She was mobbed wherever she went. Women copied her hairstyle, her simple manner of dressing, the pearls she frequently wore. Job offers bewildered her. Why would someone think that simply riding in an airplane qualified her for a job with a corporation? she wondered.

Her father seemed of the same opinion. He said:

> She was headstrong. I was strongly opposed to her flying. I am inclined to think it's just a sporting adventure. She was always inclined that way, first with automobiles and motorboats, now with planes. She is also interested in boxing and has ridden horses a great deal.

This all boils down to exactly what she so often said, nothing to make a fuss over. It was Captain Railey and George Putnam who persuaded her to play along with the wave of fame, to let it put her in a position to make other flights that would ease her conscience. What would she do if she turned her back on this opportunity? Go back to social work, eking out barely enough money to take an occasional hop around the Boston skies?

No. Common sense alone dictated that she ignore her pride, accept what she considered unearned, and forge on to prove herself later. She was an amateur suddenly catapulted into the orbit of accomplished explorers and trailblazers. She could either fade out overnight or keep on flying and work

Amelia Earhart, circa 1928

hard to hone her skills. And in that way perhaps she would chalk up later some real accomplishments more to her liking. She gritted her teeth to the accolades of the world and set out to turn herself into a real professional.

While hobnobbing with celebrities and being greeted like a superstar didn't give her great pleasure, Amelia did get satisfaction from the simple fact of having shown that women could do something if given the chance; that they were not the hysterical types everybody thought; that they, too, had courage and endurance; that they too deserved to dance on the world's stage. George Putnam must have shown her this side of her fame, which allowed her to finally accept it and let it become part of her life.

As for Putnam, he diagnosed: "AE belonged to that small class created by a combination of chance and courage whom mankind may be said to make and pay for being its heroes."

Day by day fame changed Amelia Earhart. While Kansas City, Chicago, Atchison, Des Moines, and Boston claimed her as their native daughter, she found that the family she left behind on that takeoff from Newfoundland she had left behind for good. No longer could she tell her mother or Muriel everything. Now she had to be careful of what she said even with them for fear they might unwittingly repeat her words to the press. Neither woman could truly understand her new world, so she gave up trying to explain it.

And what of Sam Chapman—now of Marblehead, Massachusetts, a lawyer with Edison Electric—who hoped one day she'd settle down and marry him? Sam did not fit into her new life. But George Putnam did.

Putnam filled the gap left by the absence of her family and the world Amelia never came back to. He became her couselor, business adviser, promoter, and confidante. "After the pleasant accident of being the first woman to cross the Atlantic by air," she said, "I was launched into a life full of interest." Putnam was there beside her all the way from the very beginning.

"Don't wear that silly hat," he'd tell her after spotting a photo of her in a newspaper. "Buy something that looks like . . ." Not only did he tell her what to wear, he also counseled her on what to say and how to say it. Remember, keep smiling because a serious face in photos comes across as a glum one, he taught her. She never forgot, and passed along the lesson to her mother. Before taxiing to a hangar after a historic landing, Amelia quickly removed her goggles, smoothed her hair, and started smiling.

Money accompanied the newfound fame. A newspaper syndicate bought her rights to *The Friendship* flight story for $10,000. As agreed, she turned that money over to *The Friendship* treasurer to help pay for the flight expenses.

But she did get the chance to make money she could keep. Lucky Strike solicited her endorsement of its cigarette brand along with that of the two men, Stultz and Gordon. Although she neither smoked nor drank throughout her life, she agreed so that she would have money ($1,500) to give to Commander Richard Byrd for his next South Pole expedition. When that cigarette ad appeared, the public went into an uproar over their clean-cut, all-American girl associating with the evils of smoking. One fan sent the ad with a note to her saying, "I suppose you drink, too."

McCalls Magazine, which had offered AE a job as aviation editor, retracted the offer. George Putnam instantly got *Cosmopolitan* to make Amelia an even better offer for a similar spot.

Gone was Amelia Earhart's privacy. Everywhere she went, crowds besieged her, clamoring for autographs, taking photos, asking questions. Mail came to her by the stacks, much of it asking for money, some offering marriage proposals. Nonetheless, as George Putnam noticed early on, "She had a quality of spirit which fame could not disturb."

Putnam's publishing company commissioned her to write a book about *The Friendship* flight. Lindbergh's book *We* had been one Putnam publishing coup; now, having "Lady Lindy's" account, as the press had dubbed her, would be another. Somehow Putnam convinced Amelia to stay with his family in Rye, New York, so that she would have the privacy to write. Celebrities did not dictate into tape recorders then, nor were ghost writers brought in to make real-life accounts sound glossy. People wrote about their own exploits, sitting down and putting words to paper themselves. This produced personal accounts of experiences as they were truly seen and felt by some of the most fascinating personalities in American history.

The luxury and peace at Rye made Amelia's task go quickly and easily. The result was the book *20 Hrs. 40 Mins.*, a recounting of the flight. At the same time, Amelia was writing articles for *Cosmopolitan* on aspects of flying.

When September came, the book was done and a lecture tour arranged by Putnam lay ahead. In the free time she had before the tour, Amelia Earhart decided to take off in her Avian Moth and just fly.

There was no Sam Chapman around to talk her out of flying cross-country this time. After covering the Atlantic, she would be forever beyond anybody's knowing better than she what was best for her to do. She had the money and the plane, and she was ready to break loose. Armed with maps, she headed west.

Landing in a grass field at Pittsburgh, she hit a ditch hidden by weeds and wound up hanging upside down from her seatbelt. **AMELIA EARHART NEAR DEATH IN CRASH**, headlines screamed. Unhurt, she continued westward after some minor repairs to the Moth.

She intended to spend as much time in the air as possible in order to bring her skills up to the level of her acclaim.

Her map flew out of the open cockpit at one point on the trip as she was hand-pumping gas from a reserve tank. Lost, she was finally forced to land on the main street of a tiny town that turned out to be Hobbs, New Mexico. The Avian's wings could be folded back (like a true moth) and that night the plane sat parked at the side of the street.

Reaching Los Angeles, Amelia watched the start of national air races. Several days later, she turned her own propeller east toward home, or what she used to call home for a while. For where was her true home anymore but in the air?

Over Utah, her engine failed. For the second time on this trip, she was forced to make a "dead stick" landing, which meant she came down without power. Unhurt, she continued on her way soon after. Amelia Earhart's luck held, as was not always the case with other pilots.

Off on a lark, happy-go-lucky in her planning, Amelia nonetheless set another record: first transcontinental solo by a woman going from East Coast to West Coast, and back again.

Perhaps because the Avian failed her so often on that trip, she wound up selling the small plane in the spring of 1929. She acquired a larger, more dependable plane—a used high-wing single-engine Lockheed Vega.

That June, her sister, Muriel, married. With a schedule squeezed tight with lecture commitments booked by George Putnam from his New York publishing office, Amelia missed the rehearsal in Massachusetts and the prewedding party. However, she did arrive in time to be maid of honor for the service. At once, she flew off again.

Again the West Coast lured her, this time to participate in the first air race for women. The route went from Santa Monica to Cleveland, Ohio. The race results were based on elapsed time and no night flying, so stops were made each day at prearranged airports.

Humorist Will Rogers kicked off the race with jokes, which gives some idea as to how the derby was regarded even by its officials. Rogers termed the contestants "ladybirds." Newspapers picked up his tone, poking fun, calling the race a "lipstick derby," the women "flying flappers," despite the fact that they were serious aviators, and the dangers for them were as real as for any male pilot.

One woman was killed when she encountered engine trouble and her parachute failed to open after she bailed out. Others ran into mechanical difficulties. As for Amelia, she crashed into a sandbank at the second stop, but her propeller was only slightly damaged, so she managed to stay in the race. Out of 19 women, 15 finished. First place went to Louise Thaden, second to Gladys O'Donnel, and third to Amelia Earhart.

The fact that she did place gives some indication that her flying abilities were improving. That fall she quit her job with *Cosmopolitan*. Shortly after, she set a speed record for women over a mile course. Then, with Ruth Nichols' help, she was instrumental in calling together a group of women pilots with the idea of organizing them.

They called themselves the 99s because there were 99 charter members at first. They came together on November 2, 1929, at Curtiss Airport in Long Island, New York. The women elected Amelia as their first president, Louise Thaden national secretary.

Busily Amelia continued to rush from one lecture commitment to another. Women in the audiences never tired of hearing her talk about flying. Among other topics, she outspokenly discussed flying safety, whether mothers should allow their daughters to learn to fly, or wives let their husbands fly on business trips. "I am at home in the air," she said, "many others, if they aren't today, will be tomorrow."

Transcontinental Air Transport (TAT), granddaddy to today's TWA, was formed by ex-Army flier Gene Vidal, former mail flier Paul Collins, and Amelia, who was their chief source of publicity as she traveled the country making speeches. They offered a cross-country service, considered fast for its day, that allowed a passenger to leave New York on a Monday night and arrive in California on Wednesday evening. An offshoot of TAT was the Ludington Line, a Northeast corridor service much like today's shuttle. From TAT, AE moved on to the Boston & Main Airways, always encouraging others to travel by plane.

Wherever she went, George Putnam was in touch by mail. To reply, she wrote in the margin of his letter and sent it back.

From the start, George Palmer Putnam must have been fascinated by this blunt, unassuming yet capable and handsome woman who did not try to court his favor as most women would and did. Amelia found him intriguing, as she told Marian Perkins at Denison after that first meeting before she was chosen to fly the Atlantic. And in those weeks before *The Friendship* took off from Boston, George Putnam was a constant companion, sometimes with the rest of the crew, sometimes alone. When she got back to the States, successful, acclaimed, he proposed marriage. She refused.

The fact is that Putnam was already married, and to a woman Amelia liked: Dorothy Binney Putnam. Mrs. Putnam was AE's hostess during her stay in Rye, and the person to whom Amelia dedicated her first book. The Putnams had two sons. Amelia dedicated the book, perhaps pointedly for George's benefit, to her hostess for the duration of her stay in Rye.

However, George Putnam was a man who went after what he wanted, and usually got it. He could sell almost anything. He was a writer, explorer, editor, and an extremely successful publisher. He had been mayor of a small town in Oregon for seven years after striking off on his own with $300 in his pocket. He led expeditions for the Museum of Natural History and wrote books about them. In all, he produced 10 books, four on travel, four biographies, and two novels. His son, David, went along on the trip to Greenland and while still a child wrote a best-seller called *David Goes to Greenland*.

GP's grandfather, father and uncles were deans of American publishing, socially top line, men of enormous wealth and influence. Against a man with these qualifications, Sam Chapman would seem to stand no chance.

On the other hand, GP had drawbacks. Tall, dark haired, rather stern looking in rimless glasses, he had an unpredictable temper, but that wasn't the worst. Though his social position would seem to be secure, at times he still acted like an overeager social climber, seeking out celebrities to invite to his home, with an eye to exploiting the situation. He loved the spotlight, and reporters complained that whenever they tried to take a picture of Amelia, he was right there in it. "Lens louse," they called him. The brashness, the advantage seeking, the con artist type that made him a successful promoter alienated him from most people.

Somehow none of this bothered Amelia Earhart. She was able to see the good in him, and perhaps, since they were both adventurers, they understood each other. GP was her Svengali. She was the talent. He was the barker. She was the show. They needed each other. They worked together. Yet there were times when she put brakes on his schemes, basically keeping her own counsel. Nobody took that away from her.

Without Putnam, Amelia Earhart might have disappeared from sight after *The Friendship* journey, and the swarm of other women pilots eagerly buzzing into the skies would have grabbed the prizes she nailed down for herself. To be a hero in an heroic age required cold cash, and nobody knew that better than George Putnam. That's what he taught his protégée, Amelia Earhart, and that's what he made available to her with his guidance and promotions. His role in creating the indelible heroic figure of Amelia Earhart and in carving it into the national psyche cannot be underestimated.

In 1930, when Putnam and his wife divorced, Amelia eventually said yes—or rather nodded yes—to GP's sixth proposal of marriage. She patted his arm, as if to reassure him, then strode out to her Vega. Her decisions appeared to be made quickly, but most often the elements of them had been brewing in her for some time. Then when she was ready she moved with no glance back.

Her decision to marry was more frightening to her than any decision connected with flying. Marriage seemed like a cage to someone who, as George Putnam described her, needed freedom the way plants need air to survive. The idea of any kind of cage was terrifying to her.

As for himself, GP said: "AE knew me better probably than anybody else ever can. With her discernment, why she married the man she did was often a matter of wonder to me. And to some others."

Captain Railey opposed the marriage. So did Amelia's mother. Her grounds were that Putnam had been married before (divorce being a stigma then) and was 10 years older than her daughter. Railey's objections are less clear. Rumors said he, too, was in love with Amelia but chose to remain with his wife.

Whether the death of Amelia's father in the fall of 1930 influenced her ideas about marriage is impossible to say. However much he had failed her and the family, though, Edwin Earhart was a man she had always loved. His death was a blow.

In February 1931, at George Putnam's mother's home in Noank, Connecticut, Amelia Earhart married George Palmer Putnam. The bride wore a brown crepe blouse, brown lizard-skin shoes, and brown suit and went hatless. The clothes were not new. Before the service, she handed her husband-to-be a note signed AE.

"I feel the move just now as foolish as anything I could do. I know there may be compensations but have no heart to look ahead . . .

"I must exact a cruel promise and this is that you will let me go in a year if we find no happiness together. I will try to do my best in every way."

Clearly this was no blushing bride. She was 33 years old but still fearful of confinement, of anyone who might try to clip her wings. With her note she hoped to protect herself. She did not tell her mother of the wedding. Amy heard about it from reporters who pestered her for her opinion on the match. Diplomatically, Amy said that if her daughter was happy, she was happy. It was not until two weeks after the ceremony that Amelia wrote to tell her mother that she was happier than she expected to be.

Amelia's ideas on marriage were far ahead of their time. In her opinion, wives should contribute money for expenses, if not for any other reason than that it kept a balance of power between the two people. She also thought that too many women used marriage as a retreat from personal failure, or as a way to avoid taking responsibility for themselves. She kept her own name, which was so rare at that time that newspapers, notably the *New York Times*, insisted on calling her Mrs. Putnam anyway. GP never referred to her that way, but always as Amelia Earthart, and, in fact, he learned to laugh at being called MR. Earhart.

There was no honeymoon. Amelia flew off on a publicity stunt, touring the country in an autogyro with BEECHNUT GUM painted on the side. In the process she set an altitude record for autogyros, the forerunners of today's helicopter.

As for George Putnam, he went on to promote her career unstintingly. Having a wife who paid her own way and pooled her money with his suited him fine. Other women fliers experienced twinges of envy thinking she was now able to buy the latest, most expensive equipment because she had married into wealth. Actually, Amelia's Vega, which she paid for, was replaced by Lockheed during a checkup when it was found to be beat up to the point of being unsafe. AE, through lecturing and promotional stunts and endorsements, paid for her flying.

"Women should be able to seek as unrestrictedly as men any gainful occupation their talents and interests make available," she declared. And her husband, George Palmer Putnam, agreed. This marriage was to be no cage, but a partnership through which both were able to build and grow.

Typical roles were turned around in this match. Putnam admitted that when it came to worrying, he was the worrier sitting at home while Amelia was off flying. He demonstrated

George Palmer Putnam and Amelia Earhart

this graphically in Detroit. On her way back from California in the autogyro, she crashed on landing. GP ran toward her across the field, fell over a support wire, and broke three ribs. Amelia was fine.

Her lectures focused increasingly on feminine issues. She called for the repeal of laws that discriminated against women—as well as those that pampered them. "Wages should be based on work itself, not on sex," she said, a notion that sounds old hat today but was then revolutionary. Some people resented her ideas as well as her presence in the cockpit of an airplane, and at least twice attempts were made at sabotage.

After a year, she and GP remained married. The matter of her wedding note to him does not seem to have been discussed again.

"Ours has been a contented and reasonable partnership," she told people, "he with his solo jobs and I with mine." She cared for, lived with, and worked in tandem with the man that so many people found unlikable. And with George Putnam, even her mother had to admit, Amelia Earhart seemed happy.

They consorted with the rich and the famous, from movie stars to presidents, including Franklin and Eleanor Roosevelt.

By 1932, Amelia had written a second book about flying called *The Fun of It*.

Still she was restless. Her future presented two basic choices: trade on the laurels of her past by playing things safe or risk all.

"I must have known for at least four years really that she wanted to . . . fly the Atlantic solo," George Putnam acknowledged. He must also have known that eventually even that challenge would not satisfy her restless spirit and quest for adventure.

"She had a quality of imaginative daring that was to wing her like an arrow," said Hilton Railey, who had discovered her for *The Friendship* trip.

6

FLY ON
Atlantic Solo, May 1932

> The project involved a gamble . . .
> My stake in this throw . . . was my
> life against the joy of doing some-
> thing I wanted to do very much.
> Amelia Earhart

The 1930s saw a burst of activity on the part of women pilots all over the world as they raced to set flight records and outdo one another. This must have put great pressure on AE to do something outstanding. Here she was a widely touted spokesperson for aviation while other women accomplished record journeys. With so many showing daring and courage, Amelia ran a real danger of being left behind if she didn't find some way to outdo everyone.

The Great Depression gripped the nation. Millions of people could not find work. Soup kitchens and bread lines were part of the national scene. The entire world was experiencing economic collapse.

Hard times didn't effect Amelia Earhart, though, as she continued toward her goal of pushing on in aviation wherever she found an opening. She was still obsessed by the notion of proving that she was not a phony hero.

In 1929, Americans Bobbi Trout, age 23, and Elinor Smith, 17, both set endurance records aloft. Britain's Amy Johnson soloed England to Australia in 1930. Ruth Nichols of the United States broke AE's transcontinental speed record, then went on to set a new altitude record as well. On a roll, by 1931 Nichols led the world pack of women pilots in both speed and altitude. She looked to be the likeliest contender to take on the big challenge still facing women: solo across the Atlantic, following Lindbergh's example.

Ruth Nichols announced she would make the attempt, and set off for St. Johns, New Brunswick, where she would refuel before making the long solitary haul across the ocean. At St. Johns, however, she crashed on landing and broke five vertebrae. A plaster body cast didn't stop her from flying home, vowing to try the Atlantic again soon. But weather turned bad and the trip had to be put off for a month, then two. While waiting out the weather, Ruth Nichols challenged France's Marie-Louise Bastie's nonstop transcontinental mileage record of 1,849 miles set earlier in 1931. En route from California to New York, her airplane caught on fire. Nichols escaped just before the gas tank exploded, somehow managing to free herself despite the difficulty of moving about in the plaster cast. Now her plans to solo the Atlantic had to be put off indefinitely. She had to find ways to raise funds to replace her demolished plane.

That left two possible contenders in the United States: Amelia and Elinor Smith, who backed out for financial reasons, leaving the field clear for Amelia Earhart in the spring of 1932. It was either attempt the trip then, when the Atlantic winter storms had died down, or someone else was sure to try again soon.

Still, when people pressed to see if she planned to take on the Atlantic, Amelia put them off, saying she wasn't ready yet, she needed more flying experience. Secretly, she was assessing her skills to determine if she was indeed ready.

Meanwhile, under her guidance, the 99s organization was working to help and promote women flyers by gathering and providing information about jobs and keeping records of their feats. Today this organization continues to play a key role in women's aviation.

To some of her fellow 99ers, Amelia Earhart let down her guard enough to admit that she still felt like a phony, that *The Friendship* trip and the fame that followed still tasted bitter in her mouth. Perhaps it was this feeling more than anything else that pushed her to the decision in 1932 to fly the Atlantic.

A year after marrying George Putnam, she told him of her decision over breakfast.

Over the past four years, she had logged nearly a thousand flying hours, many of them on instruments alone. She practiced setting courses, estimating arrival times, then setting out without looking around to check her position on the way. This skill was essential if she were to cross the Atlantic with nothing but the ocean below.

With Putnam's help, she set up a timetable. They decided what had to be done before takeoff day, and agreed to bring in an expert to help prepare her and the airplane for a successful completion of the journey.

Bernt Balchen was their first choice. A flier, explorer, and adventurer, he had accompanied Admiral Byrd to the North and South poles. Marriage to Putnam, as well as fame, gave Amelia the access to such experts as Balchen that many other women did not have.

Balchen came to lunch on one of the first days of spring in 1932. Crocuses bloomed on the lawn where they adjourned for a game of croquet after eating. It was there that Amelia told him what she wanted.

"Will you help me? Am I ready?" she asked.

"Yes," he responded to both questions.

Criticisms had been leveled about her lack of flying expertise at the time of *The Friendship* trip and shortly after. Her abilities were not at the level of Wilmer Stultz, a fact she herself pointed out frequently during the hullabaloo that followed her first Atlantic flight as a passenger. This criticism, along with society's attitude that a woman always needed some man at the controls of an airplane, must have made her doubt herself even more. Female pilots were referred to as "fair devotees of flight," implying that they were not equal to men in the air.

Even though Amelia had flown coast to coast without any man's help, placed in a transcontinental air race, and set altitude and speed records, society still regarded women as incapable of real aerial achievements. The public fawned over her for things she considered unimportant, at the same time they downplayed her real accomplishments. By actions, she hoped to let other women see the truth apart from society's opinions.

Her plane needed a new engine. This one would have twice the power of Lindbergh's *Spirit of St. Louis*. For the long flight without refueling, it needed extra gas tanks. To oversee the work, Balchen had the plane moved to the Teterboro, New Jersey, airport across the Hudson River from New York City and near where he lived. He hired Ed Gorski, engineer and maintenance supervisor for Fokker, to undertake the alterations. Getting the proper fuel mix was crucial. Helping with that project was Army pilot Major Edwin Aldrin. (In the 1960s, his son Buzz would make America's second voyage to the moon.)

The trip was kept secret in order to give Amelia the freedom to back out at any time, and also so that she could prepare herself mentally without interruptions. Officially the plane was chartered to Balchen to keep her name out of speculations about the work he was performing in connection with the craft.

The plane's flying range with added fuel tanks was 3,200 miles. From Harbor Grace, Newfoundland (the jumping-off point) to Paris, France, would be a distance of 2,640 miles. The added fuel tanks gave Amelia a safety margin of 560 miles, thus allowing some room for headwinds or losing her way.

While Balchen worked on the plane, Amelia flew when she could, and visited Doc Kimball at his weather office in Manhattan. His expertise had been crucial to *The Friendship* flight and now, though Amelia didn't reveal her intentions, he cooperated fully with her. Her keen attention to weather patterns in the North Atlantic told him all he needed to know.

Weather would play a big role in this long flight, since planes then were fragile and incapable of flying above storm systems that were miles high. Predicting weather in those days was more guesswork than science, but Kimball did his best with guesses. Sometimes storms over the North Atlantic covered the entire distance between Newfoundland and England.

"The doing of a thing may take little courage," AE wrote later for *Cosmopolitan Magazine.* "The preparation for it—the acceptance of the inevitable risks involved—may be a far greater test of morale."

Throughout the first part of May, storms raged over the Atlantic keeping her from leaving.

Then came Wednesday, May 18.

Thursday, May 19. GP drove to Manhattan. Amelia drove to Teterboro Airport for a routine visit. Fog coated her windshield. The Hudson River lay under a thick haze.

Just before noon, as she prepared to take off for a quick hop in the Vega, a call came. It was GP at Doc Kimball's office. Weather was breaking. It would be clear to fly as far as New Brunswick that day. Then, GP told her, "The Atlantic looks as good as you are likely to get it for some time."

The trip was on. "OK. We'll start."

She raced back to Rye, changed into flying breeches, a windbreaker and leather flying suit. She grabbed $15 in cash, some maps, and a toothbrush. As she hurriedly left the house, the sight of spring flowers struck her. "Those sweet blooms smiled at me a radiant farewell," she wrote later. "That's a memory I have never forgotten." The excitement, the razor's edge of danger, made her senses keen.

Four years of preparation had brought her to this moment when she would be on her own at last, ready to prove to herself—and the world—that she was nobody's phony.

Putnam met her en route and together they drove to Teterboro, arriving at 2:55 P.M. By 3:15 Amelia Earhart, Ed Gorski, and Bernt Balchen were airborne and heading north to New Brunswick. Balchen flew the plane so that she might rest along the way. After a stopover at St. Johns, New Brunswick, that night, they took off early in the morning of May 20 and flew on to Harbor Grace. From there, when she got the OK from Kimball about the weather, Amelia would be on her own.

Putnam's cables awaited them. A storm system lay to the south. Winds, out of the west, were favorable. That night would be clear, with a moon. There were some clouds 400 miles east.

If Amelia didn't get away that same day, weather might close in again for a long while. "Under these circumstances," she said, "it was harder to wait than to go."

She decided to leave that afternoon.

A 12-motor German flying boat, the Do-X, lay at anchor 24 miles away in Holyrood on its journey to the Azores, from where it could feed weather information to Harbor Grace. Amelia decided not to wait for that assistance. She wired GP that she would leave at 5:00 P.M., then lay down while Balchen and Gorski gave the plane one last check.

"In anything that requires intelligence, coordination, spirit, coolness and willpower, women can meet men on their own ground," she once said. But words were nothing without proof. She was soloing for all women.

Bernt Balchen warmed up the red plane with the gold stripe down the side. A cable arrived from New York. OK STOP SO LONG STOP GOOD LUCK. GP. This was the language of explorers and adventurers that Amelia and George Putnam shared, an understatement in the face of danger.

Heavily loaded with gasoline, the single-engine Vega would require skilled handling on takeoff. Balchen gave Amelia last-minute instructions: what course to hold, what weather she might expect. Wind ruffled her blond hair. She bit her lip as he talked, anxious to be going. It was close to 7:00 P.M. before she got away. Her beloved Vega waited for its greatest challenge and she hoped she "would not let it down." "Do you think I can make it?" she asked Balchen with what he later described as a "lonely smile."

"You bet," he said firmly. They shook hands. Twilight approached as she climbed into the cockpit of the airplane and started the engine. After checking the instruments, and without glancing from her control panel, Amelia Earhart nodded to Gorski to remove the chocks from the wheels. Slowly the red and gold plane began to roll down the runway, then finally turned, and paused. The vastness of the sky and the ocean beyond lay before this woman whose most distinguishing physical characteristic, according to her husband, was her slimness. The small red plane thundered and shook as the motor revved for takeoff. Then, throttle shoved to the firewall, it came roaring down the runway. The waiting, the preparing were over.

"The plane picked up speed quickly," the New York Times said of her takeoff afterward, "and before it had rolled 2,000 feet down the runway it had left the ground . . . Nursing the engine carefully she climbed and went into a wide turn over Lady Lake and out across town over the blue waters of Conception Bay."

Balchen, Gorski, and airport manager Herman Archibald scrambled up a cliff near the end of the runway to watch the single-engine Vega, NR-7952, with the scarlet tail fin vanish into the distance.

"To . . . do a thing for its own sake, to enjoy doing it, to concentrate all one's energies upon it, that is not only the surest guarantee of its success it is also being true to oneself," she had written.

When George Putnam received word that his wife was on her way, he called a news conference. **"PUTNAM SURE OF WIFE'S SUCCESS,"** the Times said. And: **"FIRST WOMAN TO MAKE ATTEMPT FACES CLOUDS 400 MILES OUT BUT PLANS TO SOAR OVER THEM."**

A reporter asked Putnam how he felt. "As well as could be expected," he replied.

At one hour out, her log notes two icebergs in the water below. Two hours: a small boat. She blinks her lights but gets no response.

In Newfoundland, Gorski and Balken waited for reports from ships that might have spotted her. They heard nothing. Her estimated arrival time in Paris was 12 to 15 hours after takeoff. There was no means of communication with the plane en route since radios were not part of her plane's equipment at that time.

Sunset over the North Atlantic lasted those first two hours, then the moon rose as clouds began to form below. Suddenly the needle of her altimeter spun. In 12 years of flying, it had never broken before. Now without it, she would have no idea of how high or low she was flying. Ahead, visible in the moonlight, spread a towering mass of black clouds across the horizon as far as she could see. With no way around the approaching storm, Amelia Earhart headed into it. By 11:30 P.M. the moon had vanished, blotted out by blackness. Surrounded by seething black air, her only light came from the dim glow of the instrument panel. The storm struck.

Lightning split the dark as winds knocked the plane about and rain lashed it. The plane bounced and jolted, thrown by violent forces. It was a storm worse than any she had ever encountered. Still, calmly she went about resetting her Sperry gyrocompass every 20 minutes as planned, even though she knew she might already have been blown off course.

At times such as these, she found comfort in doing small, practical tasks.

The moon reappeared at a break in the clouds. Thinking she might be able to get over the turbulence, she began to climb, the plane nosing upward. Temperature in the cockpit dropped rapidly. Slush began to collect on the windshield. Her airspeed indicator turned erratic and began to spin. This meant that ice had to be forming on the wings, making the plane too heavy to overcome the force of gravity. The controls felt sluggish in her hands. A moment later, the plane rolled over and fell toward the earth.

Plummeting through the storm, Amelia Earhart struggled to pull the plane out of its high-speed spin toward the ocean. Down it screamed. How close was the water? How far had she climbed? When would she hit? Picking up speed as it dropped, the Vega fell 3,000 feet, a fact recorded on the barograph on board, before, at the very last second, she was able to pull it up when she could see whitecaps. There was no time to enjoy her relief. The storm closed in and she could no longer see again, though she knew from that one glimpse that the water couldn't be more than 100 feet below.

"It gave me a queer feeling not being able to know when I was getting too near the water . . . I had to fly low to prevent ice forming but I certainly didn't want to go into the Atlantic."

These experiences would have been enough to make most people turn back, but she flew on, perhaps believing the worst had to be over. What more could happen?

Flames broke out through a crack in the manifold ring. In her book *The Fun of It* she later wrote that she was sorry she noticed the flames because they looked so much worse at night than they would have appeared in the daytime. The plane began to vibrate fiercely, as though any second something was going to break and send her falling into the icy waters. Perilously close to the point of no return, she still had enough gas to take her back to land if she turned around.

It was then, reported the *New York Times*, she made her bravest decision: to fly on. "If she went ahead it meant fighting wind and rain in mid-ocean with a partly crippled engine. She decided to go on."

Actually should she have turned back, she would have been trying to find Newfoundland in the dark, which was chancy, and land in the dark, which was extremely risky. This was a flight she had undertaken with little thought of aborting it along the way.

In the cold and sitting tensely in one position for so long, her feet grew numb at the rudder pedals. The storms continued to buffet her about as she changed compass settings regularly, keeping watch for any signs that she was getting close to the water below.

If the engine didn't fail on her, she decided she still had a *fair* chance of making land the next day.

The forecast turned out dramatically different from what was predicted. Atlantic weather conditions change rapidly. By the time Doc Kimball got reports, they were already old. Though he was as careful and painstaking as possible under the circumstances, there was a wide margin for error. Ironically, the very trouble Amelia waited so long to avoid engulfed her.

Past the point of no return, she continued heading east. Now there was not enough fuel for returning, only enough to take her to her destination. Guessing, she flew what she hoped was high enough to avoid the water, yet low enough to keep ice from forming on the wings.

When interviewed for a women's needlecraft magazine, Amelia had been asked, "Do you spin?" "Surely I spin," she replied, "tail spin—at 4,000 feet."

There was no way for her to rest or sleep. For food, she punched holes in the top of a tomato joice can and sipped at it still unable to see where she was going, as she plowed on through the "soup."

In the night, her fuel gauge broke. Gas leaked down the back of her neck, filling the cockpit with fumes that made her nauseous and her eyes water.

"In moments of danger," she wrote later, "whether you are coward or hero, you do your best."

Without being able to see anything out her windows but turbulent blackness, Amelia Earhart flew on for over 10 hours. Dawn came. The light revealed heavy clouds above and below. Gradually the plane's vibrations had worsened and Amelia did not know, because of the broken gauge, how much fuel she had left.

"Morning was the worst," wrote Muriel in *Courage Is the Price*. "Seeing mirages, seeing 'land' that wasn't there."

The plane shook so hard that Amelia forced herself to give up the notion of trying for Paris. She had to seek out landfall as quickly as she could. Since Kimball's forecast had noted storms to the south of her course, she thought that perhaps she had been blown south into them. Therefore, after giving up on Paris, she altered her course to due east hoping to find Ireland. The plane spewed flames, shaking so hard that at any moment it seemed it might break apart. Having flown out of touch with the world for over 13 hours in violent winds and storms, AE knew she would be very lucky indeed to find any land at all.

Each minute that passed must have been agonizing, because she did not know what the next minute or hour held. When she saw a black line on the horizon, she had to doubt her hopes that it was a shoreline; but as she flew on toward the line, it did not vanish like the dream of a desperate pilot, but grew and grew. It became mountains. It became water breaking on a shore. Railroad tracks finally appeared. These were the last moments of the crossing. Carefully, painstakingly, Amelia Earhart searched the rolling emerald pastureland below her for sight of a smooth, long stretch with no stones, fences, or ditches. As her plane roared overhead, cows scattered. Spotting a meadow, she throttled back to start her descent. Despite the mechanical problems with the airplane and the uneven terrain, she made a perfect landing. The plane rolled to a gentle stop at the top of a slight knoll. Motor switched to off, AE sat back to let the realization of what she had done seep into her. She had made it. Wherever she was, she surely had crossed the Atlantic.

Dan McCallon, a farmhand, came running to see what the noise was all about.

He couldn't tell if he was talking to a man or woman, since AE's face was greased against the cold, and she wore a flying suit and a leather helmet. Politely he inquired, "Have you flown far?"

"From America," came her dry and probably numb reply.

Later McCallon confessed, "I was all stunned and didn't know what to say."

Shortly after 9:00 A.M. New York time, George Putnam received a transatlantic call from Londonderry in the north of Ireland. It was his wife.

"I DID IT," she shouted.

Reports varied on the time it took her to make this flight that turned her into a real pilot in her own eyes and placed her in the American pantheon of heroes, which till then was exclusively male: Charles A. Lindbergh, Babe Ruth, and Jack Dempsey, among others.

The *New York Times* stated she had flown 14 hours, 56 minutes. She said the trip took 13:30. Some sources today say her time was 15:18. Whatever her time, she had clearly broken a 16:15 record set in 1919. Not only was Amelia Earhart the first woman to wing her way alone over the Atlantic, but she did it in record time. She was also the first woman to fly across it twice.

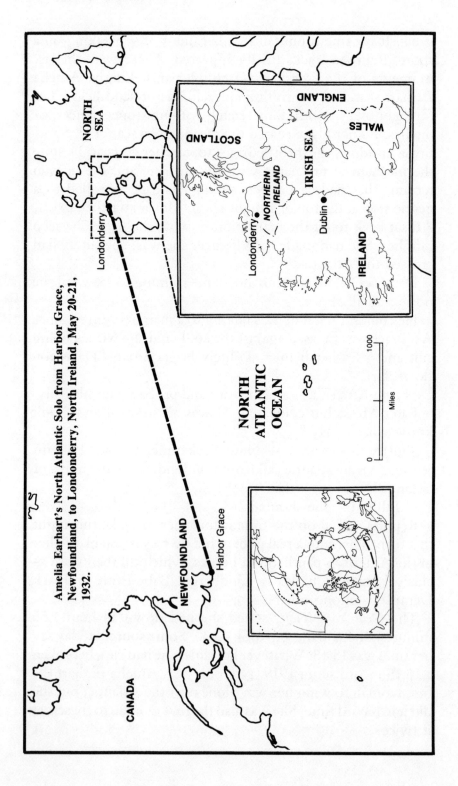

Amelia Earhart's North Atlantic Solo from Harbor Grace, Newfoundland, to Londonderry, North Ireland, May 20-21, 1932.

That Sunday, May 22, the *New York Times* ran a two-column headline:

MRS. PUTNAM FLIES ATLANTIC TO IRELAND IN RECORD TIME; DO-X REACHES THE AZORES.

Faye Gillis Wells, AE's friend and a past president of the 99s, has pointed out the difference between this and the full-page headlines given to Lindbergh's takeoff. On his landing in France, the whole front page of the *Times* covered his story. In addition, by referring to Earhart as "Mrs. Putnam," the *Times* was using a name she had not assumed and was not known by, plus they tacked news of the German flying boat Do-X onto the same headline.

But, says Wells, Amelia was concerned only about doing a good job; this is what meant a lot to her. Rather than sit back and demand equal treatment, she went out and showed that she was the equal of any man. No matter how the headlines read, her actions spoke louder than any of them. With this solo she proved that women didn't have to take a back seat to anyone when it came to choosing what they wanted to do.

President Herbert Hoover cabled: "YOU HAVE DEMONSTRATED NOT ONLY YOUR OWN DAUNTLESS COURAGE, BUT ALSO THE CAPACITY OF WOMEN TO MATCH THE SKILL OF MEN IN CARRYING THROUGH THE MOST DIFFICULT FEATS OF HIGH ADVENTURE."

"I KNEW YOU'D DO IT," wired Phil Cooper, her dry cleaner in Rye, New York. "I NEVER LOST A CUSTOMER."

"YOU BEAT ME FOR THE SECOND TIME," Ruth Nichols cabled. "BUT IT WAS A SPLENDID JOB."

Yes, AE had beaten the other women who wanted to make this record, but not because she was concerned about winning out over competition so much as because the deed was there to be done. Breaking new ground was what enticed her.

"We congratulate you," the Lindberghs cabled.

Triumphantly, AE landed at London's Hanworth Airpark and posed cheerfully for photos in the drenching rain, as the world went wild with celebration over her accomplishment. The (London) *Times* wrote: "Not Americans only, not women only, but the whole world is proud of her." The *London Sunday Express* proclaimed: "A GREAT GIRL."

Greetings from the British prime minister were conveyed inside a club house where U.S. Ambassador Andrew W. Mellon and his entourage formed an official welcoming party. Then she was whisked to BBC studios to speak via radio to America.

Everyone who could get to a radio that day was listening, including AE's mother and sister who had to go to a neighbor's house to hear the broadcast. At first they didn't recognize Amelia's voice, but then she used some "pet" phrases, and they knew who it was.

Crowds wanting autographs formed wherever she went in England, as she attended luncheons, receptions, press conferences. She insisted she had done nothing outstanding but had taken on the challenge simply "for the fun of it." Flying all night isn't very much, she said. The more she protested, the more people loved her and cited her for her modesty as well as her courage.

She and GP met up in France when he arrived on the S.S. *Olympia*. The French senate presented her with the Cross of the Legion of Honor. In Italy, Mussolini received them, though the fascist dictator was baffled by a woman who wanted to be out flying airplanes along with men. Belgium's King Albert entertained them at his summer home in Laehen, where he decorated Amelia with the Cross of the Chevalier of the Order of Leopold.

Finally on June 15, less than a month after she had taken off from Newfoundland, Amelia Earhart and George Putnam boarded the liner *Ile de France* for home. Planes escorted the ship to the open sea, dropping flowers across the deck.

Ticker-tape parades, marching bands, huge crowds, and the National Geographic Society's gold medal awaited her in the States. It was the first time this medal had ever been presented to a woman.

"Mrs. Putnam," said President Hoover at the ceremonies, "has made all mankind her debtor by her demonstration of new possibilities of the human spirit and the human will in overcoming barriers of space and the restrictions of nature upon the radius of human activities." Hoover was battling national economic problems at that time, and no doubt welcomed the chance to preside over a happy occasion.

Mrs. Hoover later confided to the press that if a woman were to fly the Atlantic and set records, she was glad that it was "such a lovely and intelligent person."

With her soft voice, Amelia Earhart attempted to dampen the acclaim with her responses: "I think that the appreciation for the deed is out of proportion to the deed itself . . . I shall be happy if my small exploit has drawn attention to the fact that women too are flying."

Brushing aside her protests, a joint session of the Senate and House of Representatives awarded her the Distinguished Flying Cross.

"Unwomanly," some critics sniped at her. Some called her flight an act of "useless courage." Some complained about her short hair or the fact that she wore trousers, but nobody dared question her bravery, which was obvious.

Actually someone from her camp, Bernt Balchen, did tell reporters that he had advised her against leaving when she did. This might have struck her as a kind of betrayal, and which also provides a glimpse at another side to her character that was to emerge later and figure most importantly in her destiny—impatience. (She once told her sister, Muriel, that it took too long to have a baby.) When she was planning this solo, Balchen told Amelia to wait, that there was too great a danger of ice forming on the plane this early in the spring. But she wouldn't listen. She was eager to go.

No doubt the fact that she was to fly on the same day that Lindbergh had undertaken the flight five years earlier also made her determined to proceed. For a man to urge her toward caution when another man would not hesitate to fly was something to which she reacted with sensitivity. Above all, she did not ever want to fall into timidity, and went out of her way to avoid any show of "weakness."

She told an audience at Kansas City, "It might burn slowly [the fire in the plane] and do no harm for the next 12 hours, or it might bestir itself and burn a part in two and wreck the plane. But there was nothing to do but fly on. If I had a boding fear of entering an airplane, I should have abondoned aviation long since. But I like to fly. So what do I know of courage anyway?"

Rear Admiral Richard E. Byrd said of her, "I know of no man who has more courage than she."

7

THE WATERSHED YEARS
Record Breaking, 1932-1937

> She is a good child, unspoiled . . . We
> have flown a lot together, my child
> and I. Sometime soon I am going to
> get her to fly across the sea with me.
> Which sea? Oh it doesn't matter
> much.
>
> Mrs. Amy Otis Earhart

Life became even more hectic after Amelia Earhart's solo that brought her to a landing on Irish soil.

"GP's schedules for her were backbreaking," Faye Gillis Wells remembered. Mrs. Wells was a friend of AE's, and a president of the 99s for a period of time. "She was changing trains in the middle of the night, going to breakfast meetings, luncheons, afternoon teas; from one thing to the next and she did that for years. She did it because she needed the money. He [Putnam] organized things so she didn't complain too much."

At the same time, the 1932 Atlantic flight that put Amelia Earhart solidly in the annals of aviation and American history sent her winging on to new records, to greater achievements, and inevitably to the most demanding journey of all—around the world.

Other choices, other chances had been turned aside with the passing of years until there she was, age 34, as she is still seen in photos today: hair tousled, face wrinkled in a grin, looking girlish in her leather flying jacket and slacks.

Amelia visited the Los Angeles Olympic Games that summer. Flying back nonstop Los Angeles to Newark, New Jersey, she set a speed record of 19 hours 5 minutes.

It was time for overhauling the battered Vega, so Amelia reluctantly sold it to the Franklin Institute in Philadelphia for $8,000. From Philadelphia, the plane eventually moved to the Smithsonian Institution in Washington, D.C., where it can be seen today, the small red airplane that carried Amelia Earhart across the Atlantic and across this country, both in record time.

That same year, 1932, Franklin D. Roosevelt defeated Herbert Hoover for the presidency. In office he launched his New Deal to combat the economic Depression. George Putnam had a knack for making friends in high places, and he and Amelia became friends of the new president and his first lady, Eleanor. In April Amelia wrote her mother from the White House, where she spent the night. Once Amelia took Eleanor on a flight over Washington, and would have taught her to fly, too, but the president said no.

July 1933. Amelia and Ruth Nichols entered the Bendix coast-to-coast air race, the only two women in a field of men. This was a breakthrough for women. They flew the same course at the same time, but they competed for a separate prize so that they wouldn't be in direct competition with the men. Amelia came in third overall, beating Nichols by an entire day, then turned around and zoomed back to Newark nonstop, breaking her own speed record of the year before by two hours.

At the end of 1933, France's Fédération Aéronautique showed Amelia Earhart leading the women of the world in aeronautical records. French flyer Maryse Hilz was second.

During the Depression day-to-day survival itself was a struggle for most people. As a result they lost interest in aviation. Besides, they were getting used to the idea of airplanes and barnstormers. Pilots joined air races and attempted new and more difficult feats, forging routes over previously uncharted territory, primarily to keep the public's attention.

In January 1934, a fleet of U.S. Navy planes pioneered a flight from the West Coast to Honolulu, Hawaii. Suddenly the Pacific, with its vast expanse of water, became an area for aviation's next challenges.

This would be her next solo, Amelia told her husband. Not from California to Hawaii, however, but the other way: west to east—because "it will be easier to hit a continent than an island," she said.

What Amelia set for herself that time had never been done before by anyone—man or woman: solo from Hawaii to the U.S. The journey would require 14 compass course changes alone.

She and George rented a house in California that fall, a move that placed them right in the center of the booming aviation industry, which had focused itself on the West Coast. Paul Mantz, who would be involved as well in the round-the-world flight later, was hired as technical adviser.

Mantz was a daredevil flier, a Hollywood stunt man who flew in GP's movie called *Wings*, which won an Academy Award for best picture of 1928. Mantz was a risk taker, but only when the risk was carefully calculated. (He faked college credentials to qualify for the Army Air Corps.) When it came to piloting and aviation equipment, Mantz expected precision.

So preparations began for this fresh venture. At the same time, she kept on lecturing and making personal appearances

L'AÉRONAUTIQUE D'AUJOURD'HUI

Ruth Nicholls (Etats-Unis).   Lady Heath (G.-B.).   Maryse Bastié.   Amelia Earhardt (Etats-Unis).   Maryse Hilsz.
AVIATRICES

Famous women pilots of the 1930's

around the country. As always, her schedule was one that would exhaust most people.

Wherever she went, she was instantly recognized. A highway patrolman stopped her for speeding, saw who she was, and insisted she come home to meet his wife. In Pennsylvania, George and Amelia were plucked from a restaurant by the town's firefighters, who invited her in to ride in their fire truck.

The flapper era was over. People criticized any reminders of it, including Amelia's short hair and her wearing of trousers in public. Because she once endorsed Lucky Strikes, people often still assumed that she smoked, and that subject frequently came up as well. Angered by the comments, she snapped, "Why shouldn't I smoke if I want to?" and lighted three cigarettes at once. "There—I smoked," she declared. And never did again.

Two altimeters were installed in her new Vega to prevent a recurrence of what had happened over the Atlantic when the instrument went out, leaving her unable to tell how high or how low she was flying. While Amelia studied maps, a route chart was prepared—two and a half feet long. Each part covered one compass setting. Mantz asked for two possible landing sites in California: Los Angeles and San Francisco, depending on which one she was near on arrival.

Preparations were tedious, painstaking in their accuracy. On these figures and graphs, her life would depend.

A fire at Amelia's home in Rye, New York, convinced the couple to make their home permanently in California, and this they did in the fall of 1934. Amelia's mother, Amy, finally came to spend some time with them. She was there at the house when Mantz, his wife, Amelia, GP, and mechanic Ernie Tissot set sail for Honolulu on the S.S. *Lurline* shortly before Christmas. Amelia sent a Christmas cable to her mother from on board. The Lockheed Vega, specially outfitted for long distances, lay lashed to the ship's deck, and drew a great deal of attention, especially whenever AE started up the engine.

Again she had attempted to keep the upcoming trip a secret, but on arrival in Hawaii, she was surrounded by reporters, who had figured out the story before she ever arrived. She insisted she was simply there to fly around the islands. Nobody really believed her, but she was dutifully quoted all the same.

Then word of the flight leaked to the press, bringing criticism from both the U.S. government and the public.

The plane had been moved to the Navy's Wheeler Field because of its long runway. This was imperative since the plane would be heavy with gasoline and slow to lift off. The Navy, however, protested that her radio equipment wasn't adequate to guarantee flight safety, that its range was only 300 miles. As a result, they refused to give her clearance to take off from Wheeler.

In response, Mantz simply took the plane up to 12,000 feet, then contacted a radio station in Arizona over 3,000 miles away. The Navy backed down.

As for the public, they were tired of stunt pilots trying things that endangered their lives and might cost a great deal of taxpayers' money should a search become necessary. This had happened as recently as November 1934, when Captain Charles Ulm and two other men left California for Honolulu and were never seen again. For 27 days, the Coast Guard, Navy, and Army searched for the downed ship. The last to give up the search was the cutter *Itasca*, which would figure prominently in Amelia's flight around the world three years later.

The fact that Amelia proclaimed quite openly that she flew "for the fun of it," although she also professed the hope repeatedly that her ground-breaking flights would open the way to commercial routes soon after, didn't sit well with the general public at this stage. To spend money trying to find a pilot who was attempting something risky didn't make sense to the populace in 1935, many of whom were living in poverty.

The greatest criticism of all came from U.S. businessmen who felt threatened by the Hawaiian sugar industry. GP had convinced Hawaiians, primarily sugar growers, to put up $10,000 as a prize for AE if she successfully completed her Honolulu-California flight. The favorable publicity this would bring to the island was not all the donors had in mind.

Though this wasn't part of the agreement, the Hawaiians no doubt also hoped the publicity would draw attention to the debate going on in Congress at the time about whether to reduce U.S. sugar tariffs. American businessmen resented what they regarded as an intrusion by a U.S. public figure into commercial matters. They charged that Amelia was "selling her soul for sugar," an accusation that no doubt stung her.

Nobody had anticipated such an uproar. The Hawaiian backers panicked. In a meeting at the Royal Hawaiian Hotel just four days before the flight was to take place, they voted to withdraw the prize.

Amelia Earhart made a surprise appearance at that meeting. Looking every inch the pilot she was, in her leather jacket and jodhpurs, she made a dramatic stand, one that was both bold and strong. Instead of pleading or apologizing, she attacked. "There is an aroma of cowardice in this room." She didn't mince words. There was no justification to the charges that the Hawaiians were trying to unfairly bias the U.S. lawmakers, she pointed out, but if the Hawaiians ran out on the deal now, they would make the accusations *seem* true.

She was there on their island to make this historic flight, she went on to say, and make the flight she would—with or without their support. (This was a gamble. No doubt she and Putnam both counted heavily on that $10,000 to pay for the enormous expenses incurred in this flight and all its preparations.)

With so much opposition to her making the trip, AE became all the more determined to do it. "I assume all responsibility for the flight," she told the men in Hawaii. "Whether you live in fear or defend your integrity is your decision."

At once the Hawaiians switched their vote to one of confidence in this brash golden-haired woman. The prize was reinstated. The trip—if successful—would have the pot of gold awaiting Amelia Earhart at its end.

Now all she needed was the right weather forecast. That was much slower in coming than the businessmen's change of heart.

During the two weeks of waiting, Army engineers overhauled the Vega. Its fuel capacity was expanded with additional tanks so that it wound up with a capacity of 525 gallons, which, it was estimated, would leave the plane with "a few gallons of gas to spare," by the time it reached the United States.

More safety equipment went on board for this flight than for her solo across the Atlantic: an inflatable rubber raft was stowed, though in a difficult place to reach. A hatchet and knife were added in case she went down and had to chop through a part of the plane's skin to reach the raft. That she would have time to accomplish such a feat in the event of an emergency is hard to imagine.

Also on board would be a flare pistol and a life preserver. When asked if Amelia would take any other emergency gear, George Putnam merely shrugged and said, "What else would she take?"

January 11, 1935. The wind blew at gale force and before noon light rain turned into a downpour. Amelia rested at the home of Mantz's friend Chris Holmes, where they were staying, while her husband and Paul Mantz drove to the airfield to check on the plane and the weather forecasts. Early afternoon arrived and the rain turned into a light patter. Putnam was told that another weather system was moving in from the west. If Amelia wanted to get out ahead of those storms she must leave at once.

As the rain ended, she donned her brown fur-lined flying suit and headed for Wheeler Field. By the time she got there, the weather had cleared enough for takeoff.

George Putnam was sweating. "I would rather have a baby," he told the few reporters who gathered nearby.

She would be pushing eastward on the heels of a retreating storm system, but it was either that or wait perhaps another two weeks to leave, so Amelia Earhart was eager to get into the sky.

Wheeler Field was not paved. Its thick grass was soggy from the rains. By the time Amelia arrived the wind had died to less than a whisper. A row of white flags marking the runway hung limp, as did the windsock. No wind meant it would be especially hard to become airborne. Even under normal circumstances, takeoff in mud was hazardous, but with the heavy load she would be carrying in the Vega, takeoff called for a great deal of skill.

Mechanic Ernie Tissot warmed up the Vega. This would be Amelia's first long-distance trip with a radio on board, giving her the capability of sending and receiving spoken messages. It had a transmitting capacity of 50 watts. Her call letters were KHABQ, and her day frequency was 6210, night 3105, the same frequencies she would use two years later on her trip around the world. Like the previous plane, this one was painted red with a gold stripe down each side to make it easier to spot in the water.

A year before to that day, January 11, 1934, six Navy planes had arrived in Pearl Harbor from San Francisco, inspiring Amelia Earhart to make this solo hop on which she was about to embark. While the crew of those planes celebrated this anniversary in Honolulu, Amelia Earhart climbed into her cockpit. Revving the engine, she checked pressure and temperature gauges and listened for any fault in the motor's rhythm. Perched near her, Mantz intently watched the dials one last time. Then AE closed the Isinglass hatch, and Mantz climbed down.

Shut off from the rest of the world now, alone with her aircraft and her fate, Amelia concentrated on the sound of the engine, roaring, then idling. The red plane shook like a small horse eager to be given its head.

AE signaled the cockpit, and Ernie slid away the chocks from the wheels. A wave to GP and Mantz came from the slender helmeted woman in the craft, the woman who loved poetry and who often wore pearls. The engine noise shutting out all other sounds, she slowly taxied across the field.

Ernie ran alongside, white faced, eyes wide, mud squashing up over his shoes, a cigarette in his mouth. Later Amelia said she wanted to call out "Cheer up, Ernie! It will soon be over," but he wouldn't have been able to hear her over the engine's roar.

The plane turned at the far end of the runway. Beyond it she faced sugar-cane fields, and past the fields, a jagged line of mountains, their tops disappearing into low hanging clouds. Fire engines and ambulances stood parked nearby. Along the muddy strip, Army and Navy personnel held fire extinguishers. With all that gas on board, the Vega was a potential bomb.

AE opened the throttle.

Riding in a car that careened alongside the plane, Putnam matched her speed at first. The plane rocked in the slick turf. Mud flew in all directions as she headed toward the mark where she would have to chop the throttle if she wasn't off the ground.

Standing near a white flag marker, Paul Mantz screamed "GET THAT TAIL UP." As if in response, the small plane hit a bump and lifted slightly. In that split second came Amelia Earhart's chance to shake free of gravity, to take flight. As the Vega threatened to settle back to the ground, she shoved the throttle full forward. Ever so slowly, the airplane lifted and continued to rise—2,000 feet of runway to spare.

"If I do not go a good job," she had written before leaving, "it's not because the plane and motor are not excellent nor because women cannot fly."

Even for veteran pilots like Amelia Earhart, taking off is one of the most thrilling moments in a flight, according to all reports. When she was asked what she thought about in those seconds, when the plane separates itself from the fetters of earth, Amelia said she was far too busy at that point simply handling the controls to pay attention to what she was feeling.

"No pilot sits and feels his pulse as he flies. He has to be part of the machine. If he thinks of anything but the task at hand, then trouble is probably just around the corner."

Ten people had lost their lives trying to cover the same Pacific route that she planned to traverse. No one had ever done it alone.

Amelia dipped her wings over Honolulu as Putnam hurried to radio statio KGU so that he could try to contact his wife on her radio, which, by prearrangement, she would have tuned to the commercial station's number on the band.

Amelia Earhart, aviatrix

Takeoff had taken place at 4:30 P.M. At 5:00, over Makapupu Point, the furthest tip of land, she rolled out the trailing antenna.

"Important news flash," a radio announcer broadcast. "Amelia Earhart has just taken off on an attempted flight to Oakland, California. Mr. Putnam will try to communicate with his wife."

This would be the first time they spoke to one another land to air. "Everything OK," Amelia said.

"Amelia," Putnam replied, "Please speak a little louder so that we can hear you . . ."

If AE succeeded in this flight, she would be not only the first person to fly Hawaii to California solo, but also the first person—man or woman—to cover both the Atlantic and Pacific oceans alone.

There was no moon. She flew into clouds. Then darkness came. Finally the air cleared and stars shone around her "near enough to touch." Patches of rain squalls marred her course over the seemingly endless water. Ships scheduled to be in her area along the way looked for her, sending spotlights skyward to aid her in navigation.

Her radio messages were monitored by the Navy, Coast Guard, and commercial stations. Broadcasting irregularly, she talked of the weather, her altitude, and speed but gave no position. She had to know she should tell people where she was, but she enjoyed the freedom of "being lost" to the world, of being temporarily unfindable. Free of others and their directions and opinions, there was nothing to mar the closeness she felt with her plane, the night, and the stars.

Around midnight, about 900 miles out, she spotted a bright star. That turned out to be a searchlight from the ship *Maliko*. They blinked lights at one another. There was rain ahead.

Dodging storms, she had to recalculate her position on the meticulous charts and in her compass settings, constantly refiguring, and then having to refigure all the other headings as well, since when one was changed, they all had to be altered.

Relaxed, she ate a hardboiled egg. Normally on long-distance flights she would eat nothing. The beauty of this flight particularly moved her, and beauty had always been one of the reasons why she loved flying. At times, she mentioned on the radio that the stars seemed to "rise from the sea and hang outside my cockpit window." Most pilots, she felt, were in love with the beauty of flight.

Across America, people waited by their radios to get reports of her journey, eager for any bit of news about her progress, hoping to hear when and where she might touch down. Crowds gathered at both the Los Angeles and Oakland airports, anticipating the sight of a small single-engine plane searching for the field.

Daylight came. Three different times, she believed she had spotted land, but it turned out to be a mirage—a cloud, or a shadow across the water. Station KPO in San Francisco told her the ship she described as seeing below was the *President*

Pierce. Its position was only 300 miles off shore. A short while later she spotted what she had been looking for: land—and San Francisco Bay.

Those aboard Coast Guard and Navy vessels stationed offshore to respond to distress signals fumed over her radio broadcasts. If they had to search for her, they wouldn't know where to start. Finally, the Coast Guard vessel simply gave up and turned back toward shore—just as she was landing.

"Out of the wind- and rain-whipped Pacific," according to the *New York Times* lead article the next day, "Amelia Earhart landed in Oakland, California, at 1:31 P.M. California time."

Contrary to what the crowds expected, she did not circle, she did not act as though she was struggling to find her way. She knew where she was. Nobody noticed the small craft come in low, straight, and fast at the end of the field for a perfect landing. Not until a siren went off signaling her arrival did the more than 10,000 people realize that she had landed. Breaking through police barricades, they swarmed toward the plane, and Amelia had to shut off her engine to avoid a tragedy.

Her reception, as reported by the *New York Times*, equaled Lindbergh's in Paris. This was her first hero's welcome and it touched her deeply.

"That landing is something I shall never forget," she later wrote. "It is in the diary of my heart."

Pushing back the cockpit cover, as police struggled to restrain the mob, Amelia stood, becoming visible to those below. And then she combed her hair.

The crowd cheered and shouted. A University of California student fell in the stampede. His elbow and leg were broken. People threw bouquets of red roses. They screamed. They grabbed for her. They tried to tear off pieces of the airplane as mementos.

The trip had taken her 18 hours and 15 minutes over 2,400 miles.

"I'm a bit tired," she announced to the crowd, which hungered for her every word. "You'll have to excuse me."

Mechanics tugged the plane down the runway and into the hangar. Only then was it safe for her to climb out. She was

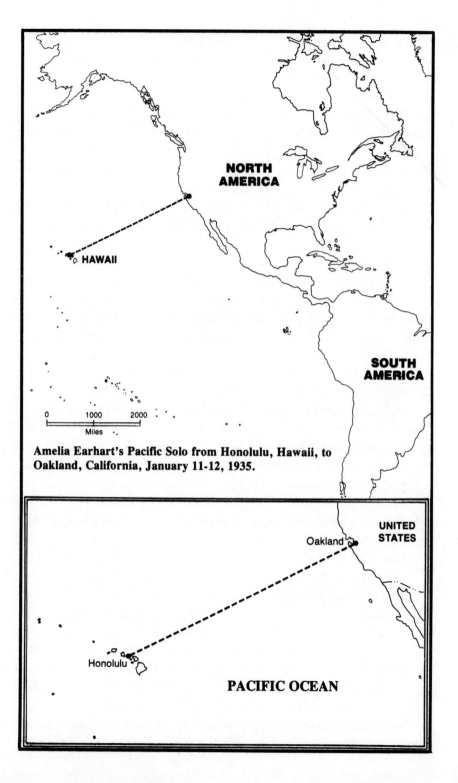

Amelia Earhart's Pacific Solo from Honolulu, Hawaii, to Oakland, California, January 11-12, 1935.

pale. Her legs trembled. "I feel swell," she said, refusing the offer of a chair. And then she quipped, "I always look this way."

Amelia attacked the many critics who had opposed her first Pacific venture. The greatest hazard of all, she told reporters, came from the negativism she ran into before leaving. "For this reason it was unfortunately more difficult than my two Atlantic flights. The criticism I had before taking off from Hawaii was entirely unwarranted and manifested itself in a physical strain more difficult than fatigue. Throughout the night, I felt this."

A waiting car took her to an Oakland hotel, where she drank chicken bouillon and buttermilk before going to bed. A guard was posted at her door. Reporters camped out at her home, anticipating her arrival there. When they spoke with her mother, Amy, she said: "Amelia and I like trying things. We like to see what a person can do. My family, the Otises, the Boston Otises, were that way. Always trying new things."

According to the New York Times, this flight made by Amelia Earhart across the Pacific was every bit as historic and monumental as Lindbergh's solo across the Atlantic. "Her speed reduced by headwinds, her course altered time and time again by towering clouds and fog, she flew her plane to hit San Francisco on the nose. It was a workmanlike job."

For her part, Amelia commented, "It seemed good training for other hoped-for long-distance flights." Already looking ahead, beyond the Pacific, she had her eyes on the world and was at the peak of her career.

On April 19 of that year, Amelia took off for Mexico City at the invitation of the Mexican consul general. The Mexican government printed special stamps for GP to buy at regular prices, which he could then resell in the United States at a profit to cover the costs of the trip. They read: "Amelia Earhart Vuelo de buena voluntad Mexico 1939."

This long but comparatively unchallenging trip nearly turned into disaster. On her way, AE's engine heated dangerously over the mountains. An insect lodged itself in one of her eyes, and at 1:00 P.M., her estimated arrival time, there was no Mexico City in sight. Sighting a flat area, she made an emergency landing. Where a moment ago there had been not a soul in sight, now there emerged Mexican cowboys speaking nothing but Spanish. After a great deal of sign language, Amelia managed to get some notion of directions. Then she had to clear a space for takeoff; it was hard to communicate to the cowboys that they should get away from the airplane.

Thirty minutes later she touched down in Mexico City, where the president of Mexico, the foreign minister, and George Putnam waited.

Concerts were given in her honor; medals presented on behalf of Mexican women. This flight added another to her firsts: first solo by anyone, man or woman, from Los Angeles to Mexico City.

This 1,700-mile Mexico trip inspired her to undertake the long flight from there to Newark, nonstop, solo. Again this would be another first.

GP arranged to have the Vega transferred to Texcoco, a dry lake bed, so that AE would have the stretch of runway she needed for a heavy-load takeoff. He then made his way back to New York City in order to relay Doc Kimball's weather information to Mexico City.

For eight days Amelia waited south of the border for Kimball's OK. Finally, at 6:00 A.M. on May 8, the weather seemed right, and with parked cars shining headlights on the Texcoco strip, Amelia Earhart roared down the bumpy course to disappear into the pre-dawn sky, heading eastward.

"As a young moon stole up into the dark arch of the sky," wrote the *Christian Science Monitor*, ". . . a handful of bright green and silver stars came out to see Amelia Earhart riding the skies once again . . ."

She climbed to 9,000 feet rapidly in order to clear the mountains that stretched out between Mexico City and the Gulf of Mexico that lay ahead.

With each spectacular flight, Amelia Earhart hammered home the message that women were competent, capable

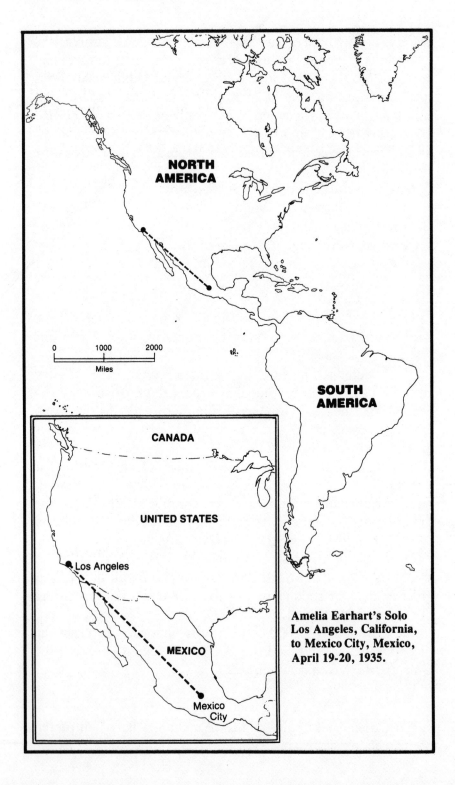

NORTH
AMERICA

SOUTH
AMERICA

0   1000   2000
Miles

CANADA

UNITED STATES

Los Angeles

MEXICO

Mexico
City

Amelia Earhart's Solo
Los Angeles, California,
to Mexico City, Mexico,
April 19-20, 1935.

pilots. Yet airplane manufacturers were still reluctant to have women operate their equipment.

Once again, on this Mexico-to-Newark trip she set a solo speed record: 2,125 miles in 14 hours, 18 minutes. She passed over New Orleans right on schedule and in radio contact with the ground. In the skies over Washington, D.C., she spoke with her friend Gene Vidal, who told her she'd flown enough, and to come down. She told him no, that she was heading on. At Newark, a crowd of thousands awaited her arrival.

"*That's* a flier," Doc Kimball told GP. "Such people are good for us all."

This year was one of repeated triumphs. Still the burdens as well as the rewards of fame rested heavily at times on this private, rather shy woman. That June she checked into a hospital for sinus surgery, the result of tension, pressure, a hard-driving schedule that brought her to the point of exhaustion.

But she bounced back quickly, especially when Purdue University invited her to join its faculty as women's couselor and aviation consultant. This school had its own airfield and a progressive attitude toward aviation. The job would require her to be on campus only one month out of the year. Also in the agreement, no doubt, was at least an indication that Purdue would play "fairy godmother" to her latest wish.

"Where to find the tree on which costly airplanes grow, I did not know. But I knew the kind I wanted—an Electra Lockheed, big brother of my Vega."

With such an airplane, she would have the mechanical capability of crossing not an ocean or a continent but the entire world.

8

WHEELS UP
Second Round-the-World Departure, 1937

> He who tries and fails may in himself
> be a greater hero than is the one for
> whom the band plays.
>
> Amelia Earhart

Amelia was piloting this Purdue airplane when the crash occurred on takeoff from Luke Field, Pearl Harbor, Hawaii. Destination: the world.

This had to be the low point of her career. One of fortune's favored ones until then, suddenly it looked as though fate might rob her of her most important dream—flight around the world.

Her previous crashes at other times paled by comparison with this one. They represented minor episodes in a period when such things routinely happened to pilots. However, this time, in a modern airplane, loaded with fuel, setting out on a course that could forever change the status of women explorers as "poor relatives in the house of the mighty," her entire reputation at stake, this crash had to be devastating to Amelia Earhart.

"I don't know what happened," she repeated to Paul Mantz, who fumed about "jockeying the throttles," as firefighters raced to neutralize the plane's gasoline which spewed out over the airstrip. "I don't know what happened," she insisted as they walked away from the Electra lying at an awkward tilt on the runway.

That romantic era of seat-of-the-pants flying daredevils was really over. It ended with the start of the 1930s. But AE didn't seem to recognize this. Her approach still reflected that time past. Fate seemed to be echoing the warning which the world had been shouting at her for some time: "Enough fun, Amelia, enough."

Usually AE tackled her flights in secrecy. They were announced only after she was en route to her destination. This time, she made known her plans the previous year. The *New York Herald Tribune* had bought rights to her serial reports from along the way. Reporters followed the preparations. Not only was this the most expensive of her undertakings to date, it was also the most publicized and scrutinized. Probably George Putnam played a key role in this promotion. However, the publicity also burdened AE with the public's expectations for performance. To back down now would be to lose credibility, to jeopardize her standing as America's premiere woman pilot.

No doubt she also felt pushed on by those many other women pilots around the world relentlessly setting their own records, earning their own medals, seeking their own places in history.

There was Jean Batten from New Zealand, who flew from England to Senegal, from there to Natal—without a radio on board because she couldn't afford to buy one. There was Marie Bastie who flew from Paris to Dakar, Senegal, and on to Natal, beating Batten's time by an hour. Also in 1936, horsewoman and trainer Beryl Markham of British East Africa, later Kenya, crossed the Atlantic from England on her way to the United States. After 21 hours, 25 minutes, she crashed at Cape Breton, Nova Scotia, becoming the first woman to cross the Atlantic in the opposite direction to Amelia Earhart's solo. Beryl Markham's book *West with the Night* was not discovered by the reading public until just before her death in 1986, which again shows how crucial George Putnam's role was in promoting Amelia Earhart's enduring fame. He made sure that people knew what his wife was doing. He got her the publicity, the interviews with reporters. Behind the scenes, he was the man behind the legend that his wife became.

At least 40 to 50 years before such a marriage arrangement became popular, George Putnam and Amelia Earhart, two strong individuals, set up their own marital rules and made their own unorthodox yet highly workable arrangement with each other. Though she is the one remembered today, her accomplishments came about through a partnership. Tirelessly, Putnam played the helpmate's part in a time when this was considered the "little woman's" role. And his efforts kept her from being ignored.

Another reason why she might have felt compelled to make this long flight: It was either that or retire.

Shrewd as George Putnam was about publicity, he must have seen that the forces that had bestowed fame upon his wife were moving on. Aviation records were becoming ho-hum. The public's interest already had turned to other things.

Indeed this last flight would place her forever in the heart and memories of Americans, but not for the reasons that she and her husband imagined.

Shortly after she made her decision to try again, she changed the routing of her next attempt. Instead of flying west, she would take off to the east since weather would be more favorable in the Caribbean and Africa on the first legs of the journey. Not until the last minute did she make these changes known to the press.

The reasons she gave the press originally when she announced the flight, in addition to simply the fun of flying, were that she wanted to study the effects of long-distance air travel on fatigue and the capacity for handling an aircraft. Did men and women differ in their reactions to flight stress? she wondered. Today these topics occupy a special branch of the new space medicine. Flying has always exposed people to extremes of temperature, noise (especially in planes of the twenties and thirties, which left pilots unable to hear anything for a while after leaving the cockpit), atmospheric pressures, and fatigue.

"I believe," her husband wrote later, "that apart from and probably much more important to her than the reasons she gave, they [these flights] represented for her the chance to be again in that universe aloft where, in a sense, she really lived."

Captain Hilton Railey, who had discovered her for *The Friendship* flight, looked at things differently. "Long before she mentioned it, I knew that next, and perhaps fatally, must come her globe-circling adventure," he said. He must have wondered—as Amelia Earhart plunged on, announcing that despite the Hawaii crash she would not give up this ambitious flight—if he had been an agent for good or ill in playing a major role at the beginning of her aeronautical life.

The second attempt, nonetheless, was on. Lockheed crews worked round the clock to fix up the Electra. George Putnam busied himself changing airfield arrangements, arranging for new visas, and raising funds. Gimbels purchased a new set of airmail covers to be sold later; they read "Second Takeoff." Functioning as a team, Amelia and George rounded up the necessary money from friends willing to back the trip with their donations. During this time, Fred Noonan got married, an event that seemed to symbolize a fresh start for him. Meanwhile, Paul Mantz continued to think he was part of the flight preparations, but since laying blame for the Hawaii crash on Amelia, he was no longer consulted.

Meanwhile the world was becoming used to the sound of churning propellers. The English now flew regular schedules to Egypt, India, the Far East, and other places. Pan Am linked up to Mexico and South America. Its Clipper route reached destinations across the Pacific, including Hong Kong. Technical improvements created faster, stronger airplanes that made all this possible. But the biggest breakthrough in air travel was sophisticated radio equipment, which pilots could use to home in on landing fields.

Tuning to a radio signal, they could take a compass bearing to follow, or receive a bearing from the landing site which picked up their position on a radio direction finder (DF).

Quite unexpectedly, Lockheed received some of this new radio equipment from the Navy for AE's Electra. Joseph H. Gurr, who had worked on the gear, did not know who was responsible for seeing that she got it. Direction-finding equipment was still experimental then, and the technology highly guarded. It could be that AE agreed to help the U.S. Navy by testing this equipment under long-distance conditions. Was

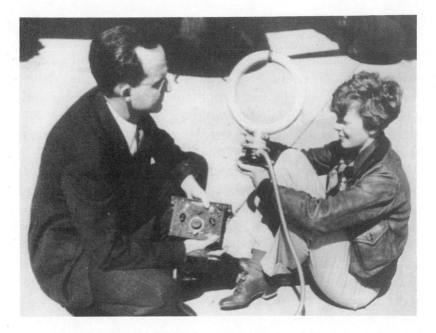

George Putnam and AE, holding a loop antenna, 193/

AE's venture government-sponsored from the start? If so, this would add a new dimension to the forces driving her on.

Before the Hawaii crash, Gurr had installed a loop antenna on top of the cockpit that could be rotated to pick up a radio signal. This would tell her the direction of the landing site, though not whether it was ahead of or behind her since she had no way to know if she had actually passed over the site already. He also installed a trailing antenna to be lowered from the plane in flight, providing a 500-kc frequency, which is the emergency SOS band used for communicating with ships at sea. Her transmitting capacity was limited but adequate, Gurr believed. Still, he couldn't get AE to take time to study how to use this equipment. She would get practice along the way, she told him.

Both she and Noonan were strictly products of the seat-of-the-pants school, and had a disdain for those who thought technology could do something better than the human mind. Once, a DF had malfunctioned on Noonan, putting off his calculations by almost 40 degrees and causing his aircraft to brush the tips of trees in a landing. If they had crashed, he told people, *he* would have been blamed, not the direction finder.

In fact, when Pan Am officials met with AE and suggested that she add a tuning radio set to a Pan Am frequency as a safety feature so that it would be possible to always know her location, she told them, "I've got a navigator to tell me where I am."

Now, 50 years after the fact, it is easy to wonder at what seems her lack of caution. But at that time all radio DF equipment was new and by no means shown foolproof. In addition, over the course of her flying career, Amelia Earhart had achieved her successes trusting her own judgment.

The radio was an intrusion on what had until then been the only place where she felt free. It started with GP telling her to "speak up" over Hawaii. She did not respond. She was on her way and no one could command her. For a while, she was captain of her fate, master of her soul—a rare and fleeting experience for her when she was on the ground.

With the original route reversed in direction, Amelia would now start out in Miami and head down through the Caribbean and along the east coast of South America.

From South America, she would make the long hop across the Atlantic Ocean to Africa. She would cross that continent's midsection to the Arabian Sea, all the while heading east and as close as she could stay to the equator.

From the Arabian Sea, she would proceed to India, Australia, Howland Island in the South Pacific, Hawaii, and finally Oakland, California.

The trip would cover 27,000 miles, calling for enormous endurance, emotional resilience, mental discipline, as well as the ability to handle an aircraft in any and all conditions. Terrains would vary widely. Weather conditions would be unpredictable. Errors could prove fatal.

Again the Coast Guard cutter *Itasca* got word to station itself off Howland Island toward the end of June. The Hawaiian-Americans who oversaw the island, and who had helped build the landing strip under the direction of Richard

B. Black of the Interior Department, moved into work sheds to make room for the fliers.

Although Amelia said she didn't want anyone homing in on *her* signals, that she would do the homing from her plane, nonetheless an experimental direction finder was sent to Howland, and Black brought in a Coast Guard radio operator, Frank Cipriani, to work it. The set was calibrated with a ship 20 miles away and it functioned perfectly. It was rigged to operate on Amelia's frequencies: 6210 and 3105 kc. They would use this set as a backup only, to get a fix on her position.

The U.S. government cooperated with equipment, knowhow, and personnel on this flight, although the assistant secretary of commerce grumbled that he would like to forbid the journey if there was any way he could do it.

Meanwhile, Putnam pressured AE to let Noonan stay behind toward the end of the flight, so that she could arrive in the States alone. She refused, saying that was when she would need him most. Jacqueline Cochran's bad feelings about the trip had not gone away. She promised AE she would use her ESP abilities to guide rescuers should her friend go down.

Two months after the Hawaii crash, right on schedule, the airplane was ready to go. AE flew it to Oakland to pick up Fred Noonan, who had been stopped for speeding not long before. A police report noted that "the driver had been drinking." There is no evidence showing that this was made known to Amelia.

They flew east with Putnam and mechanic Bo McKneely, stopping overnight at Tucson and New Orleans before arriving in Miami. Pan Am mechanics checked out the Electra for a week and Amelia worked alongside them.

"In addition to being a fine companion and pilot," Noonan wrote his bride, "she [Amelia] can take hardships as well as a man—and work like one." Amelia gained the mechanics' respect. Some of them were unhappy at first "working on a woman's plane." But her knowledge of things mechanical, her friendliness, and her willingness to accompany them to a cheap restaurant and drink buttermilk while they wolfed down hamburgers, won their respect.

Takeoff day came without fanfare. It was June 1, 1937. Amelia said goodbye to George Putnam and her stepson, David. The Lockheed Electra NR 16020 took off at 5:56 A.M. from Miami Municipal Airport. Putnam and his son waited in the control tower while she climbed, banked into a turn, and became a slender needle in the sky before vanishing from sight.

"Everything is fine," she radioed back, after turning the large plane toward San Juan, Puerto Rico. The tower tried to contact her: "Miami Radio calling NR 16020," but there was no response.

Two days later George Putnam wrote Paul Mantz describing the departure and assuring him that everything was fine. To Mantz's dismany, he learned that the telegraph key and the trailing antenna had both been left behind. The reason was that neither AE nor Noonan knew Morse Code, and Amelia considered the trailing antenna a bother. However, this meant that if anything went wrong on board, their radio transmitting and receiving capabilities might not be sufficient to handle the situation.

"Adventuring is not for novices," AE once wrote. "It is for people who have wanted to do a certain thing . . . for years . . . and who finally, concentrating on that above all other beckoning thoughts, have carried it through. . . . If you want badly enough to do a thing, you usually do it very well. . . ."

Was she as well prepared as she thought for this most perilous flight of her career? Or had she compromised her own safety in her anxiety to be off?

The Electra arrived in Puerto Rico 19 minutes off of Noonan's estimated time of arrival, with no explanation in the log. The next day, they flew to the little town of Caripito, Venezuela. Here Amelia saw a jungle for the first time.

One source reports that the manager of Pan Am's Caripito facilities wanted to turn over the latest weather and other airport information, but Amelia showed no interest. The next morning, the manager drove to the airport to talk with her but saw the plane already on its way into rain clouds.

It seems uncharacteristic of her usually disciplined handling of flights to think that she would ignore information that might be crucial. Was she overwhelmed by data at that stage—tired of advice, and simply eager to get on with the actual journey? Or did she know that she had gotten the best information possible before leaving the States, and didn't believe she needed more at this stage?

They landed in Paramaribo, capital of Dutch Guiana, now known as Surinam, on June 3. This was one of Noonan's former stopping-off places when he worked for Pan Am. His friends there told people later that Noonan had started drinking again.

The next morning, they made a 10-hour flight over jungle and ocean to Fortaleza, Brazil. There they prepared for the Atlantic crossing to come. They repacked the plane, sent home gifts, maps of routes covered, and Amelia's write-ups, which appeared regularly in the *New York Herald Tribune.*

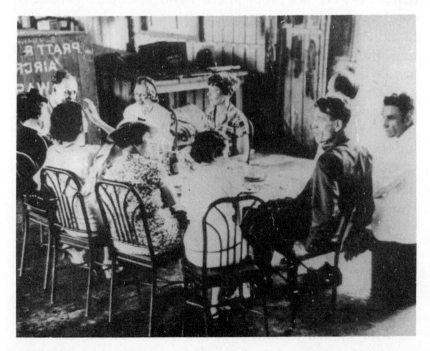

Amelia Earhart and Fred Noonan at Venezuela airport on round-the-world flight

Always the concern was with limiting the weight on board, so that they could carry the necessary heavy load of fuel.

On the streets of Fortaleza, people stared at Amelia Earhart, and the hotel tried to put her in the same room with Noonan. The plane was checked by Pan Am mechanics. On June 6 they struck out for Natal, Brazil, landing in a squall. With the long Atlantic crossing ahead of her, Amelia wanted to leave at once, but Air France pilots managed to talk her out of it. She waited until the next morning at 3:15 A.M., when she and Noonan checked out the grass field by flashlight before taking off.

Amelia's love of poetry is reflected in her logs from this trip. Putting on the Sperry Autopilot, which freed her to write, she noted such things as: "The sun illumines mystic caves or shows giant cloud creatures mocking with lumpy paws the tiny man-made bird among them."

Noonan passed headings up to her in the cockpit via the cumbersome fishing pole system. At 6:45 A.M. they crossed the equator for the second time.

"Sun brilliant, little lamb clouds below," she wrote. The sunny spell ended abruptly. They hit rain, a headwind. Gas fumes leaked into the cabin, making her stomach queasy. "Tried getting something on radio," she wrote. "No go."

Noonan dozed in the back of the airplane.

As they neared Africa, he sent up word for her to turn south. She felt that Dakar, Senegal, lay to the north. Instead of following Noonan's directions, she followed her own instincts. The trip had taken over 13 hours. She was tired, ready for a break from flying. She missed Dakar, but luckily she found a town with an airport large enough to accommodate the Electra. It turned out that Dakar was exactly where Noonan had plotted, 163 miles south of where they had landed. Why had she ignored his calculations? Had she already become angry about his drinking? Had she stopped trusting him so early in the trip?

Flying down to Dakar the next day, they rested and looked over maps covering the central African trek ahead. Wherever she landed, she found gas drums painted AMELIA EARHART, arranged for by George Putnam.

Weather ahead was unpredictable. Jungle lay to the south, deserts to the north. That meant they could encounter sandstorms, even tornadoes, and certainly great heat. This was no commercial flight path. There would be no radio beams for homing. Their maps, on which they would completely rely, were either sketchy or outdated. Since the landing fields ahead had no lights, they had to arrive before sunset. A potential danger was the heated air which provided less lift than cool air and required a fast landing. It was also likely to be turbulent.

From Dakar, they winged on to Gao in the French Sudan, now Mali, on the Niger River at the edge of the great Sahara Desert.

June 11 found them in Fort Lamy, Chad, which was then the port of French Equatorial Africa, 1,000 miles west of Gao. Part of the landing gear collapsed here in temperatures well over 100 degrees.

By 1:30 P.M. the next day, with repairs completed, they pushed on to El Fahser, Sudan, and were thoroughly sprayed with disinfectants by local officials.

"Our flights over the desert," Noonan wrote his wife, "were more difficult than over water, one part of the desert being as much like another as two peas in a pod. There were times I wouldn't have bet a nickle on the accuracy of our assumed position." Despite this lack of landmarks, they never lost their way.

The arduous trip ground on. Sunday, June 13. Khartoum, on the Nile; temperature 110 degrees. Then they took off for Massawa, Ethiopia, on the east coast, where temperatures hit 120 degrees. Next, they flew down to Assab, Ethiopia, for a two-day layover. Fifteen days had passed. Nearly half the total distance had been covered.

From Assab, the flight looped around the south coast of Saudi Arabia en route into what is now Karachi, Pakistan, but was then India. Amelia had to get special permission to skirt the Arabian coast, and carried a letter in Arabic begging for mercy in the event that she went down there.

This part of the trip went smoothly, however, and at Karachi, mechanics once again pored over the plane to make sure everything was in good working order. Here Putnam caught up with Amelia by telephone from the States. Their connection had to travel by shortwave through London, and from there to Bombay. After hanging up, AE went off to ride a camel.

The night of June 17 they took off for Calcutta. That same night the monsoon struck. Takeoff was treacherous, but AE refused to delay because of the weather. Calcutta lay 1,400 miles away across the heart of India. The monsoon winds and rain lashed Calcutta as the plane landed. Despite this, they headed on to Akyab, Burma, and landed the next day.

June 19. The Electra was forced to turn back while attempting to reach Thailand. Storms were so fierce that the rain battered paint off the wings of the plane. Visibility was zero. Noonan navigated them back to the landing strip at Akyab with great skill.

Trying for Bangkok again the next day, almost by sheer force of will, AE pushed on through the monsoon and arrived safely. She and Noonan were both exhausted. At this point Noonan's easygoing attitude collided with Amelia's discipline and drive. She was a tough captain to please, and she was pushing him hard. By then he was drinking heavily. "I don't know where he's getting it," she reported to Putnam by phone.

Right after refueling in Bangkok on June 20, they took off across the South China Sea, into the relief of clear skies and a landing at Singapore.

Relentlessly, they flew on the next day to Bandoeng (Bandung), Java (Indonesia), crossing the equator for the third time. At Bandoeng, KLM mechanics probed the plane. In a conversation with Putnam, Amelia said, "He's hitting the bottle again."

From here it was a short hop to Suribaya, Java, on June 24. But what started as an easy trip, became an aborted one, as they turned back with a mechanical malfunction. Something in long-range instruments that Noonan worked with was not responding properly.

On their return to Bandoeng, Amelia spoke again with her husband. He was on his way to California and their reunion, and had stopped off in Wyoming. Now he wanted to know the reason for their delay.

"Is everything OK about the ship now?" Putnam asked.

"Yes," she said. "Good night, Hon."

"Good night," he replied. "I'll be sitting in Oakland waiting for you."

They landed at Koepang (Kupang) on the island of Timor, Indonesia, on a grass field where there was no hangar. The Electra had to be tied down with its nose into the wind.

As they progressed eastward, they "lost time" rapidly. Soon they would lose an entire day when crossing the International Date Line.

On June 28 in Port Darwin, Australia, once again AE and Noonan were sprayed by disinfectants. Asked why she didn't use the field's radio direction finder in her approach, she replied that something was wrong with her equipment. A fuse was located as the problem—and replaced.

Her log does not explain why they spent two days at Port Darwin. From here all nonessentials were once again shipped to the States, including parachutes—and Amelia's good-luck bracelet, which she always wore on a trip. No doubt one part of her went along with the idea of good luck, and the more practical side of her felt it was just added weight. They had come 22,000 miles with 7,000 yet to go.

June 29, 1937. Takeoff for Lae, New Guinea. Here another two days passed; this time Putnam wired to find out the reason for the delay. AE wired back tersely: "Crew unfit."

Ahead lay the hardest part of the entire journey: 2,556 miles over open South Pacific waters to find Howland Island, two miles long, one half mile wide, no higher than 20 feet at any point. Specifically, for this extremely difficult job she had brought along Fred Noonan. This leg of the trip required navigational skills that few men possessed.

"In these fast moving days . . ." she wrote from Lae, "the whole width of the world has passed behind us, except this broad ocean. I shall be glad when we have the hazards of its navigation behind us."

On this section of the journey, Amelia and Noonan would need all the luck they could get.

9

MISSING
Disappearance Between Lae, New Guinea, and Howland Island, July 2, 1937

> To die will be an awfully big adventure.
>
> Peter Pan (J.M. Barrie)

The original plan had been to fly every day in order to complete this round-the-world trip in record time. Now, Lae, New Guinea, brought an additional two-day delay. The official reason given: bad weather and problems with Noonan's chronometers. If these malfunctioned when he made his calculations, it could mean a difference of crucial miles over the Pacific.

Amelia Earhart chafed at the delay. Waiting had always been the hardest part of any trip for her. Doing battle directly with the odds, tackling the situation head on, made her come alive. The longer she waited, the more costly the trip became in daily expenses, and the harder it might be to earn that money back if she missed certain deadlines in the States. George Putnam kept urging her to polish off the trip. Get on with it. This added fuel to her own hard-driving desire to forge ahead.

Still, she couldn't leave Lae without making sure all risks were reduced to the minimum. There was a 2,556-mile leap ahead to Howland Island, near the equator, and from there another giant bound to Hawaii. Once in Hawaii, she no doubt felt confident of reaching the mainland without a problem

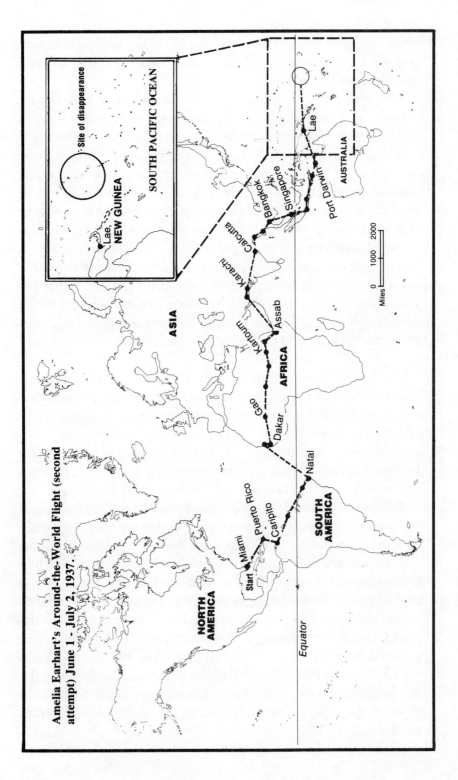

Amelia Earhart's Around-the-World Flight (second attempt) June 1 - July 2, 1937.

since she had made the trip solo in 1935. It was this section—Lae to Howland—that had always worried her and
everyone connected with the flight.

Fred Noonan's drinking had to be a worry now, too. Before
it could have been passed off as annoying; at this point it was a
matter of life and death. Or had she given up relying on him?

The extent to which she had lost faith in Fred Noonan came
to light years later when Harry Balfour, radio operator at Lae
airfield, revealed that Amelia asked him to come along to
Howland. That she considered bringing him when weight
was so crucial aboard that even her good-luck bracelet had to
be sent home shows her desperation. Or was she planning on
leaving Noonan behind? And if so, didn't she have to worry
about unfavorable publicity when the trip was over, either for
abandoning Noonan midway or taking *two* men on part of the
trip? In any event, Balfour declined. There was an air of doom
about the trip, he told people later, and that was why he would
not go.

His refusal didn't stop Amelia Earhart. With or without
Balfour she was bound to continue. Balfour was amazed that
she would make such a dangerous hop with a navigator in
Noonan's condition.

During her two days in Lae, Amelia talked at length with
Harry Balfour, setting up her own navigational checks and
safeguards so that she would be sure to find Howland.

Balfour contacted Nauru island to request navigational
assistance for Amelia. Nauru responded positively: Not only
did the island have a shipping light of 5,000 candelas
(candlepower) that could be seen for 34 miles, it also had
phosphate field lights that would be blazing through the
night. In the dark, over open water, Nauru, a tiny island,
could serve as a beacon. Once Amelia spotted Nauru, she
could check her bearings, reset her compass heading, and
proceed on a verified course. To pass close by Nauru would
take her out of the way. Her flight plan was changed to take
her in this direction. The only other way for her to find out in
flight if she was on course would be through Noonan's fixes
on the stars.

While Amelia did some sightseeing, Balfour took the Electra up for a test flight to check out the radio. He reported everything was functioning well.

Later Balfour wrote that the night before takeoff, with the weather looking cooperative for a midmorning departure, Fred Noonan went on a "bender" at Bulolo. According to Balfour, Noonan got back to his room just 45 minutes before Amelia knocked at the door to wake him. He was "put on board" with what Balfour charitably termed "a bad hangover." According to alcohol experts, it takes up to seven hours for only one drink of liquor to leave the body, and having to be put on board the airplane indicates that Noonan had not even begun to recover to the hangover stage yet.

There were squalls ahead, heavy cumulus buildup 300 to 500 miles northeast (NE) to east (E) of Lae, with scattered clouds and possible turbulence thereafter along the Electra's route. They faced a headwind of 10 to 15 knots all the way. The plane's huge gas tanks were filled to capacity: 1,100 gallons.

This was July 2, 1937, just 22 days away from Amelia's 40th birthday. At 10:00 A.M. Lae, New Guinea, time, Amelia sat in the cockpit of her beloved plane under a blazing sun and checked the sound of the engines once again, studying the needles, preparing for takeoff.

There they were: Amelia Earhart in the cockpit, a loner, used to doing everything herself, keeping her own counsel, loathe to take passengers even on joy rides; and Fred Noonan dazed at the chart table in back, accustomed to working in a well-coordinated team with a major airline. Though their basic attitudes toward aviation were similar because of the era in which they entered it, their approaches couldn't have been more different.

And in the world which they had traversed so rapidly, news of their flight was taking second place to write-ups on the opening of new passenger routes. What five years earlier would cause the entire nation to hold its breath and say its prayers now not only failed to generate great excitement but even brought a few yawns.

Yet to Amelia Earhart this flight was her Everest. Everything she had done until now led to Lae—and beyond.

And so she sat at the controls that steamy July 2 in Lae, New Guinea, having made the decision to leave there with Fred Noonan, knowing that Balfour, who could possibly have been of help, would not come. More alone than she had ever been, she revved for takeoff.

The Electra picked up speed. The runway that had been hacked out of jungle ended precipitously at a cliff which dropped away to Pacific surf far below. Lumbering down the runway, NR 16020 did not leave the ground.

Guinea Airways employees watched tensely. At 50 feet from the cliff's edge, the plane *still* had not lifted off. At that point there was no way to abort takeoff. Thundering at top speed, the Electra roared off the end of the runway and sank out of sight.

Barely skimming the waves now, its propellers tossing spray, the plane struggled to get up, a determined Amelia Earhart wrestling with the controls.

If anyone still doubted her piloting skills, they could doubt them no longer. The Guinea Airways staff praised her profusely long afterward for saving the takeoff from disaster.

Slowly, slowly, the Lockheed Electra showed signs of rising. According to Balfour, she was still only about 100 feet in the air after flying so far east over the ocean that the plane became a black dot which finally disappeared. The takeoff, said Balfour, "was hair-raising."

If AE had left before 9:00 A.M., she would reach Howland at night. If she had left after 11:00, she would pass over the Nukumanu Islands after dark. (They were the first land sighting she would make and there she would change course to head NE to Nauru. It was crucial that she be able to spot the islands.) As it was, she got off shortly after 10:00, squeezing her way through the two-hour "window." She would fly through the day and night, expecting to home in on radio signals from the Coast Guard cutter, the *Itasca*, in the predawn hours. Estimated time to make the 2,556-mile trip: 18 hours.

Out in the Pacific, the USS *Ontario* had been stationed between Lae and Howland, while the *Itasca*, with a homing beacon, bobbed directly off Howland. Between Howland and Hawaii lay the USS *Swan*.

Every day from the time Amelia Earhart left Miami on June 2 until she took off from Lae, Commander Thompson aboard the *Itasca* had been radioing for information on when AE would broadcast, what frequencies she would use, and the type of signal that suited her direction-finding device. He had been calling the Coast Guard and Navy offices in California. After many days, word came from George Putnam via the Coast Guard. He asked the *Itasca* to prepare for "possible use of 3105 kc for voice," adding that the plane's direction finder (DF) covered 200 to 400 kc.

Commander Thompson sent word to the Coast Guard to tell Putnam to tell Amelia Earhart that he would give her "smoke by day and searchlight by night," to help her find her way to his ship.

Then came another message by way of the same routing via GP, as Amelia was winging her way across the world. The message came from her and it contradicted what Putnam had radioed earlier. She sent word to the *Itasca* that her DF covered 200 to 1500 and 2400 to 4800 kc. She asked the cutter to transmit its position every half hour on 7500 kc, a frequency that, in her same message, she admitted would be beyond what she could receive.

Trying to clear up the confusion, Thompson radioed back to San Francisco that the ship could use its DF gear only between 270 and 550 kc. As though she had never been given his message, AE sent another message, this one saying that she expected Thompson to broadcast on 3105 kc, a frequency he had not mentioned, and one that would be too weak for direction finding beyond 200 miles.

This is the confusion over the radio frequencies that existed up to the time of AE's takeoff from Lae. A clear agreement between her and the *Itasca* did not exist, regarding when she would broadcast and on which frequencies she would operate her direction finder. Though Thompson was responsible at this stage for bringing NR 16020 in safely, he still had not been able to find out accurate or consistent information from Amelia, Putnam, the Navy, or the Coast Guard.

In addition, he wasn't even informed of her takeoff. He expected them to leave Lae on July 1 (Howland was one day behind Lae since it lay across the International Date Line), but he couldn't get confirmation on this from anyone he contacted. Night came. Finally San Francisco radioed that Amelia was on her way. The cutter settled in for a long night's vigil.

Boat parties were formed in case the plane came down in nearby water. The man who was to operate the direction finder from Howland, Frank Cipriani, was sent in by a small boat. (Commander Thompson didn't like the idea of having so many people in on the operation—too much chance for mixup, in his opinion.)

"Viewed from the fact that Miss Earhart's flight was largely dependent upon radio communications, her attitude toward arrangements was most casual to say the least," said a frustrated Thompson later.

Midnight arrived. The *Itasca*'s searchlights raked the sky so black it seemed impenetrable. Gooney birds that congregated on the runway were killed in an attempt to keep the way clear.

Shortly after her takeoff, Amelia spoke via radio with Balfour in New Guinea, using 6210 kc. Four hours later, KHAQQ (Amelia's call letters) crackled through again; this time she told Balfour she had run into high cumulus clouds and was going under them.

About eight hours into the flight, with Balfour still hearing her signal strongly, Amelia said that darkness had come. There was a sliver of a moon. She was about to switch to her night frequency. Balfour radioed back urging her to stay with 6210 since she came in on it clearly. She did not reply. Had she even heard him?

Word came to Balfour from Ocean Island (located just beyond Nauru) that she would be encountering strong headwinds. This would be important information for her to have in her navigational calculations, but Balfour couldn't raise AE on 3105 or on 6210, her day frequency. He was unable to speak with her again.

Modern analyses of the radio transmittals between Balfour and Amelia determined that if AE had only stayed on 6210 kc she probably could have been in touch with Lae until just before sunrise. These analyses were done by Paul Rafford, Jr., using space-age technology.

Time passed. On the island of Nauru, T.H. Cude, the director of police there who was listening on his shortwave radio at home, picked up Amelia's calls, saying that she saw the lights from the island. Nauru had no facilities for transmitting, however, so Cude was unable to respond. Presumably she corrected her course here from NNE to E. Or did she?

The area in which she flew now was filled with tiny islands, some barely volcanic tips. They were known overall as Micronesia. Following World War I, Japan had been in charge of the Caroline, Marianas, and Marshalls in this archipelago, islands that had previously been under German control. The 1919 peace conference gave Japan a "mandate" to oversee these islands, a mandate that expressly prohibited any military use of them. The whole of Micronesia was supposedly under the protection and jurisdiction of the League of Nations.

Technically the United States was at peace with Japan at this time. However, since the early 1920's military experts believed that Japan was building a military machine on its mandated islands. Anyone who was not Japanese or an islander was forbidden entry. In 1923, a U.S. Marine colonel by the name of Pete Ellis disguised himself as a German trader and penetrated the Marshalls and the Carolines in an attempt to gain information on what was happening there. He was found out and murdered by the Japanese.

In 1924, the United States passed an immigration law barring Japanese from settling in America.

At the same time, the League of Nations was losing its power and also could not gain access to the mandated islands to make sure that Japan was not militarizing them. A South Seas Trading Company was formed ostensibly by Japanese civilians, but informers said it was actually run by the Japanese

Imperial Navy. Its offices were located on Saipan, Yap, Truk, Ponape, and Jaluit in Micronesia. The Aslito military airport on Saipan, built in 1930, was camouflaged and given the innocuous name of South Sea Bureau Agriculture Farm No. 5.

By 1933 Japan had withdrawn from the League of Nations. A 1936 coup in Tokyo failed, with the result that the Japanese military gained even greater control in that country. To many U.S. analysts, Japan and the United States were on a collision course in the South Pacific.

Into this powder keg area Amelia Earhart flew as she winged her way toward the *Itasca* and Howland. She had to have known she could not safely stray north of the equator in this zone since northern equatorial waters belonged almost exclusively to Japan.

The *Itasca* continued to prepare for her arrival, checking its radio equipment by calling San Francisco. Reception was OK. Its message was also picked up by ships throughout the Pacific.

Shortly after midnight, the *Itasca* began to broadcast weather and homing signals to KHAQQ on the chance that AE might be able to pick them up by that time.

Wind was out of the east. The ocean was calm.

At 2:45 A.M. the cutter picked up a message almost indistinguishable because of static. "Cloudy and overcast," said a low, calm voice. Reporters from the Associated Press and United Press on board the *Itasca* identified it as AE's.

At 3:45 A.M. AE radioed: "Overcast. Will listen on hour and half hour on 3105."

Meanwhile the *Itasca* kept up its broadcasts on the hour and half hour. Chief radio operator Leo G. Bellarts, wearing headphones, struggled to hear her. Then he plugged the radio into a loudspeaker and men gathered in the radio room to listen. Bellarts radioed back" "What is your position? When do you expect to arrive Howland?"

There was no answer.

On the island itself, Cipriani was trying to pick up a bearing from those first signals coming from KHAQQ, but AE did not stay on the air long enough for him to take a bearing.

At 5:12 A.M. she called in saying she would whistle into the radio so they could take a bearing on her. Unfortunately, with all the squeaks and squawks and static that accompanied radio reception at that time, it was impossible for either Cipriani or Bellarts to distinguish AE's whistle from just plain noise. If she had continued to speak for at least two minutes, or if she had transmitted Morse Code by key steadily for that period of time, they would have been able to pinpoint her location.

There was still no response to the *Itasca*'s radio messages. The ship did not seem to be getting through.

Frustration began to build in the radio room. The latest weather report showed squalls to the northwest, where the Electra must have been.

By 5:45 A.M. her signal was much stronger. She reported "position doubtful," about 100 miles out, according to her calculations.

7:45 A.M. The entire cutter was filled with tension. There had been no two-way communication between ship and airplane. Now AE broke in, her voice distinct but sounding strained. "We must be on you but cannot see you. But gas is running low. Have been unable to reach you by radio. We are flying at 1,000 feet."

To be flying that low didn't make sense when trying to spot something as small as Howland Island. It would be easier to spot from a higher altitude. The only reason people could think of later was that AE had come down in order to get out of a storm.

Since dawn, the *Itasca* had been sending black smoke from its boiler which should have been visible for 30 miles in all directions.

By the time 7:45 arrived, Cipriani on Howland had just about given up on using his direction finder. Batteries drained, it was nearly unusable. Due to the power of AE's signal, however, everyone knew she had to be close by. But where?

7:46 A.M. The *Itasca* immediately called back. "Received your message, signal strength 5. Go ahead." And they sent out the homing signal. The Electra had been aloft now for almost 20 hours.

"We are circling," AE radioed back at 7:58 A.M., the calls coming in rapid fire now, "but cannot see the island. Cannot hear you. Go ahead on 7500 kc."

There was shock in the radio room. No ship or plane could take a bearing that far up the frequency band. Nevertheless, in desperation, the *Itasca* broadcast on 7500. At 8:01 the Electra responded.

"We received your signal but unable to get minimum." (This had to do with the working of the DF, which entailed finding the direction of *no sound*, or *null*, by rotating the roof antenna. This minimum, or null, was the compass reading for the destination. The only thing the minimum didn't give was whether the site was in front or behind.) "Please take bearings on us and answer on 3105 kc with voice," AE concluded.

This was now the critical period. With gas low and being close to her destination, AE needed radio direction finding to take her to Howland and nothing else would help. Said Joseph Gurr, who installed the Electra's radio equipment, "Amelia knew that DF was vital to the operation at Howland, therefore we must assume that the equipment on board was functioning properly before leaving Lae, New Guinea. Knowledge and accurate and precise use of DF was needed now, and there was a failure."

At 8:45 A.M., 21 hours into the flight, AE's voice broke into the radio room. To those gathered, she now sounded panicky.

"We are on line of position 157-337. Will repeat this message on 6210. Wait. Listening on 6210. We are running north and south."

Not knowing what this figure—157-337—referred to (it could have applied to any spot on the globe), the *Itasca* waited for her call to come in on 6210. It did not come.

Her signals had steadily grown stronger up to the 8:45 call. Had she gone beyond Howland, they would have gotten weaker, but they did not. This led Thompson to believe that AE might still be west of the island, and it was in this direction that he finally ordered the *Itasca* to search, when they heard no more from KHAQQ.

During all this period, she never reported her position. She also did not report having radio trouble, except for commenting repeatedly that she was not getting any calls from the cutter (save for that single message she sent between 8:00 and 8:03).

Nobody could even begin to guess where she was when she reported her position as 157-337. What was her point of reference? Some assumed that Noonan had gotten a reading from the sun, but that information, as he must have known, was useless without the reference point. Those figures gave a navigational line from nowhere to nowhere in the vast reaches of the Pacific.

The *Itasca* radio room was in a state of dread and confusion. They continued to broadcast as the cutter set out to the northwest.

Before this flight, AE had told friends that if she couldn't find Howland Island, she would probably try to locate an island with fresh water on it. With the amount of gasoline she should have had left, she could conceivably have made it as far west as the Gilberts, or if she was north of the equator, she might have reached the eastern edge of the Marshalls. In any event, heading in those directions, she would have been in Japanese territory.

Jim Collopy, district superintendent for civil aviation in New Guinea, wrote in his official report, "I can see no reason why Amelia and Fred could not have made it back to one of the atolls that dotted the Pacific along their route."

Years later Harry Balfour, baffled by the lack of radio communication between Coast Guard cutter and airplane, lamented, "Why didn't the [*Itasca*] crew 'voice' the homing signal?" which it sent by Morse Code. Perhaps they did not realize that AE not only didn't know Morse Code, she had left the telegraph key behind in Florida. Was this the reason why she couldn't pick up their signal?

And what of Fred Noonan? Even if he were hung over, he was still a crack navigator. And despite his distrust of radio DF equipment, how could his celestial calculations have led them so far wrong, unless they ran into tremendous storms? If his instruments were in order, he should have been able to determine position by the stars, and, when it rose that morning, the sun.

Or had Amelia ignored his directions that came up to the cockpit via the fishing line, as she had done before when they approached Africa?

A typhoon was now kicking up in the Carolines. Turbulence was spreading rapidly over a wide area. Amelia Earhart and Fred Noonan had vanished somewhere in a 450,000-square-mile expanse of ocean averaging a depth of 16,800 feet.

As the *Itasca* plowed through the water, vital questions haunted the commander and the *Itasca* crew: Why couldn't Amelia hear their broadcasts? What happened to Noonan's famed navigational skills? And why did Amelia suddenly stop broadcasting? *What happened?*

10

ENDLESS FLIGHT
An Epitaph

> If you go high or far enough, some
> place the sun is always shining.
> Amelia Earhart
> from *Last Flight*

Commander Thompson ordered radio signals to be continued throughout that first day while he searched. Black smoke poured from the boilers on the off-chance that AE might be in a position to spot it. That night, once again the *Itasca*'s searchlights shone into the sky.

The next day a Navy battleship, the USS *Colorado*, set off from Hawaii to join the search, and the *Itasca* was ordered to stand by off Howland. There it was locked in by a tremendous storm.

"Waves were turbulent. The monsoons were building up rollers 4–6 feet high. The impact of a plane," said Commander Thompson, "crashlanding on the breakers would shear off the wings and crumple the cockpit like paper. There would be no time for launching a rubber raft, nor any possibility of it staying afloat even if free of the wreckage."

Back in California, Paul Mantz assessed that the two on board the plane had about "one chance in a thousand" of surviving if they came down in the ocean, a difficult feat even for someone accomplished in amphibious landings.

George Putnam cabled that the airplane could stay afloat for an indefinite period of time since the gas tanks had been specially sealed to provide for flotation.

For three days after AE and Noonan vanished, radio SOS signals on 3105 kc were picked up by amateur, military, and commercial radio operators. Hoping she might still be alive, station KGMB in Honolulu radioed a message on July 4 asking AE to signal if she heard their broadcast. Both Coast Guard and Navy stations in Hawaii did hear a radio response to that plea.

In California, ham operator Walter McMenamy, an engineer with Patterson Radio Corporation, said he heard Amelia broadcasting the Friday that she vanished, saying, "KHAQQ SOS southwest Howland."

On that same day, the Coast Guard reported unidentified "carrier waves" (radio signals) from the Howland vicinity. Flares were seen during those first nights after her disappearance, but when ships investigated the areas during daylight hours, they found nothing.

Lockheed reported that the plane had to be on land in order for the radio to operate. Both Putnam and Paul Mantz contradicted this, saying the radio *could* transmit from the water. Joseph Gurr, who installed the radio equipment, said he made sure Amelia could transmit from water in the event of just such a disaster.

Meanwhile, the minesweeper USS *Swan* was also sent in to assist in searching the Pacific waters, and on July 9 the aircraft carrier USS *Lexington* with its complement of 63 airplanes, along with four destroyers (the *Perkins*, *Cushing*, *Lamson*, and *Drayton*), set out for Hawaii to help.

They did not reach Howland until July 13. From there the *Lexington*'s planes scoured the north and west. Permission was asked of the Japanese for the Navy to visit Palau, Truk, and Saipan to look for Amelia and her navigator, but permission was refused. The Japanese said they were sending out their own search vessels.

Many of the SOS messages picked up had centered in the area around the Phoenix group of islands to the southeast. Flyers who knew Fred Noonan believed he would head that way in an emergency, knowing he would find no land to the direct north. However, no indication was found of the airplane in the locations pinpointed by the radio calls.

Fruitlessly, U.S. vessels crisscrossed the South Pacific. The search cost over $4 million but the Electra was never found. There was no trace of the ship, not even an oil slick.

On July 18 the search was called off. The *Lexington* was ordered back to the United States. "Termination of mission without success" is the way their return was officially phrased. Passing under San Francisco's Golden Gate Bridge, the *Lexington* flew her flags at half mast.

Though massive, the Navy response had been sluggish—a matter of closing the barn door after the horses had run away. The Coast Guard and Navy seemed ill prepared to respond quickly to the emergency. By the time additional ships reached the area, the fate of Amelia Earhart and Fred Noonan had already been sealed.

Perhaps in defending themselves against criticism, military men jumped to the conclusion that Amelia Earhart had panicked and dived into the ocean out of sheer fright. But never had Amelia Earhart shown a tendency to panic. In fact, it was just the opposite. Even under great strain, she showed a coolness and a capacity to make reasoned, careful decisions. Naturally she must have been frightened when she couldn't find Howland, but with her skills, her experience, her personality, panic was unlikely.

With radio operators all over the Pacific and even in the States claiming to hear Amelia's distress calls, why couldn't the military locate her? The Navy labeled ham operators "quacks." Pan Am DF records were ordered destroyed. They were saved by a quick-thinking office employee of Pan Am, but it is not known where they are today. Possibly they would indicate signals from the downed craft which would show that it could have been found by someone else, namely, the Japanese.

From the moment she heard that Amelia had been lost, Jacqueline Cochran tried to put her ESP to work. George Putnam pleaded with her to do what she could to try to locate his missing wife. Meditating, Cochran was able to picture the plane adrift in the water. She saw Noonan with a fractured skull . . . AE alive. Cochran told George Putnam that she could visualize the *Itasca* as well as a Japanese fishing vessel nearby.

Putnam sent her descriptions to the search vessels. Because of the long distances involved, communications between the ships and Putnam in California must have necessarily been frustrating and inefficient.

For two days after her friend disappeared, Jacqueline Cochran repeatedly conjured up mental visions that followed the movement of the searchers as well as her friend in the water. On the third day, Jacqueline Cochran gave up.

She went to a Los Angeles cathedral to light a candle for the souls that she believed by then had departed their bodies. From that time on, she forsook ESP, saying that if it had any value whatsoever, it should have helped her save Amelia Earhart.

What did go on inside the Electra in those last hours over the Pacific as AE concluded that something was terribly wrong with either her radio equipment or with the way she was handling it? Unable to pick up a signal from the *Itasca*, she would have to rely on Fred Noonan's directions. Did she?

From where he sat in back of the airplane, he might have been prevented from taking bearings because of stormy weather. He had only one small side window for taking sights. Then, too, the method of communication between him and his pilot was awkwardly slow and did not facilitate any lengthy messages and certainly no discussion. For Fred Noonan to reach the cockpit meant crawling through an extremely tight space over the gasoline tanks. Decisions had to be made rapidly once Amelia fully realized that she would not reach her objective.

Much has been made of Fred Noonan's drinking, but after 21 hours, though he might not have felt well, he had to be sober. Unless, of course, he brought liquor with him on the airplane. However, barring that, his personal history, too, makes it hard to imagine that he could not figure out a proper course. Even if they did encounter storms, as many believed they did, he had been able to plot a course and get them back to airfields safely in the midst of zero visibility during the monsoon over Burma. There appears to be no reason that he could not have done the same thing in this situation.

If, as experts today say, finding their way in those final hours depended solely upon radio bearings, then that rudimentary equipment on board could have failed to provide a clear signal for AE to follow. Pilots of that time say it was sometimes almost impossible to pick out a DF signal from amidst the static, and the messages AE sent the *Itasca* were almost indistinguishable at times because of noise. For Amelia to pick out the *Itasca*'s homing signal, much less determine where that signal was weakest, could have been impossible under stormy conditions.

In a paper presented to the Smithsonian Institution years later, Frederick J. Hooven wrote that he had invented an improved DF which had originally been installed in the Electra. However, it was removed before Amelia and Noonan left the States the second time because it was considered too heavy. It was replaced by a lighter weight, older model. Hooven believes his heavier device, with its finer-honed capabilities, might have saved their lives—if indeed this was where the problem lay.

This is one possible scenario: Amelia had flown for 21 hours. In terms of time alone, she should have been on top of Howland Island. But there was nothing in sight. What to do next? To continue flying eastward was suicide—the only island in that direction, Jarvis, was at least as far from the Howland vicinity as Nauru was to the west. She hadn't enough gasoline to take her that far. And straight north was open ocean.

To the south of Howland, 40 miles away, was Baker Island. If Amelia had been off her course to the south, she would have spotted Baker from the air. If, however, she were so far to the south that she couldn't see Baker, she would have to be more than 80 miles in error.

Consider her final position report of 157-337. Those who have pondered this cryptic message assume that this was a NNW, SSE line, using Howland as the point where that line intersected. Even so, it was impossible for rescuers to know whether she was north or south of Howland on that line, and given the enormous space involved in the search area, this position information was therefore useless.

Whatever Amelia decided in those last hours aloft, having repeatedly failed to connect with the *Itasca* on her radio, realizing her destination was nowhere in sight and that she couldn't fly indefinitely, she probably began flying either north or south on the position line she had given, believing that it would bring her to Howland.

But was Howland north or south of where she was? That was the crucial question for her then. She didn't have the gasoline reserves to try both directions. And how could she find out exactly where she was since obviously she was not where her compass bearings were supposed to lead her? Might Fred Noonan have plotted an alternate course at this late stage, prior to ditching? Nearing Africa, she ignored his instructions, followed her own instincts, and they wound up over a hundred miles away from where they had intended to land. So would she now trust his calculations in this emergency?

To date there is no way to know what she decided, nor can it be determined where she was or where she flew after her last radio message at 8:45 A.M.

If she had been careful in the use of her fuel, and she was known for being meticulous to the last detail when it came to engine management on all previous flights, she should have had at least four hours left, which means she would not go down immediately.

But then why did she stop transmitting? Perhaps she abandoned the radio at this point because she had had no success with it. Possibly she gave up on finding Howland and turned to search out an alternate landing site. Before leaving the United States she had been given a classified Navy document showing possible landing areas as alternates to Howland, all in the Phoenix group. There were no airfields on any of these islands, but there was clear, level ground available. She had been able to make do with just such turf in the past.

She could have reached McKean Island, one of the closest in the Phoenix group, 340 miles to the SSE. In addition, according to CBS newsman Fred Goerner who has spent many years unraveling the mystery of Amelia Earhart's disappearance, there are three reefs halfway between Howland and McKean, one of which is above water part of the day. This could have been a landing site for a crippled plane. Significantly, these reefs were not investigated by rescuers at the time.

This was one of the biggest news stories of the 20th century. One of America's—and the world's—most beloved heroines, Amelia Earhart represented a romantic and hopeful era that would never come again. Tributes to her were delivered all over the world.

Amelia's friend Captain Hilton Railey, who discovered her in the beginning, spoke sadly. She had been caught up in the hero "racket" and this compelled her to "strive for increasingly fantastic records." Equally likely is that she fit the pattern described by British psychiatrist James E. Anthony: "Mastery of one such experience usually leads [the person] to test himself again, asserting himself against ever greater odds."

Newspaper columnist Walter Lippmann wrote of her:

> All the heroes, the saints and the seers, the explorers and the creators . . . can give no account of where they are going or explain completely where they have been . . . They do the useless, brave, noble, the divinely foolish and the very wisest things done by men. What they may prove to themselves and others is that man is no mere creature of his habits, no mere . . . cog in the collective machine but that in the dust of which he is made there is also fire, lighted now and then by great winds from the sky.

In November 1937, at Floyd Bennett Field on Long Island, New York, Jacqueline Cochran spoke to a gathering of the Women's National Aeronautical Association:

"Amelia did not lose, for her last flight was endless . . . she merely placed the torch in the hands of others to carry on to the next goal, and from there on and forever."

For George Putnam who had lost both a wife and a business partner, the shock of Amelia's disappearance and the aftermath were a nightmare come true. In 1944, Anne Morrow Lindbergh was to write concerning the term "lost" in connection with pilots. "It has a special agony of its own quite distinct from death."

Putnam had previously been through the terror of false reports during his wife's flying career—one that had her cracking up after her Atlantic solo, and another that placed her going up in flames on the ground loop in Hawaii during the first around-the-world takeoff.

Then on July 2, 1937, came the last message from Howland: "Circling. Gas is running low." George Putnam had seen his wife rise, phoenixlike from the ashes of such terrible words before, but it was not to be this time. This time the report stood without correction.

In December 1938, George Putnam petitioned a court in California to have Amelia Earhart declared legally dead. He wanted to marry again. The petition stated that she "died about July 2, 1937, in an airplane accident somewhere between British New Guinea and Howland Island, the South Pacific," and it listed her estate at $27,000. In January 1939 Putnam's petition was approved and he remarried.

In 1939 war broke out in Europe. Pearl Harbor was bombed by the Japanese and the United States declared war on Japan. Planes were once more involved in military action. In Russia, women flew combat and bombing sorties. In the United States, a group of women pilots performed many dangerous ferrying missions that largely went unheralded. In fact, it wasn't until 1977 that Congress awarded them veteran's benefits. The use of airplanes in war, however, sped up the development of aeronautical technology.

As war news dominated public attention, people came to accept, though not understand, the loss of Amelia Earhart from the national and international scene.

For her sister, Muriel, and mother, Amy, who had been through the initial trauma of Amelia's disappearance, followed by many cruel hoaxes, with people claiming to know AE's whereabouts and demanding money, these years must have been especially painful. They had lost the polestar in their family, the person who was once in charge, who guided them, who supplied them with money, who seemed to have a philosophy that covered all hardships.

For years Mrs. Earhart clung to the belief that her daughter was alive. She kept a bag packed for the time that Amelia was found on some South Sea island. In it was a pair of scissors to cut Amelia's hair, which would have grown long by then, and cream for her face, which would, no doubt, be sunburned. Stubbornly, valiantly, Mrs. Earhart insisted, "I still believe my daughter lives"— a mother's way of dealing with a horror that could not be accepted.

Amy told reporters she believed that Amelia was on some sort of government mission for President Roosevelt. Eleanor Roosevelt denied this in a private conversation with Muriel. She said that she and FDR both loved Amelia too much to put her in any kind of danger.

Nonetheless rumors circulated that Amelia had been on a spy mission, that she had been commissioned to photograph the Japanese-held islands. These rumors grew when the Japanese bombed U.S. naval installations at Pearl Harbor. The fact is that AE had no training in military observation. Also she would have to fly a great distance out of her way in order to pass over any of the Japanese-held islands on her way to Howland and, too, in the middle of the night. The fact that conservation of fuel was a prime consideration also makes the idea farfetched. Still, to this day, some people continue to speculate as to the reason the U.S. government took such interest in Amelia's last flight, but no evidence has ever been found to indicate that any agreement was made between Amelia Earhart and President Roosevelt or his staff.

Tantalizing bits of information occasionally surfaced to keep the mystery alive. After World War II, Jacqueline Cochran, who was one of the first Americans to visit Tokyo after Japan surrendered, went through Imperial Air Force files looking for information on women fliers to determine their role in the war. There she stumbled across a file marked Amelia Earhart. These papers were placed on microfilm and sent to the United States. Today, neither the U.S. government nor the Japanese claim to have the file. And Cochran never revealed what was in it.

Ten years passed, 15, 20. Interest in exactly what happened to Amelia Earhart never went away. Newsman Fred Goerner followed up a lead that came to his attention in the sixties. A California nurse, Josephine Blanco Akiyama, originally from Saipan, was quoted in a small newspaper as saying that she had seen a man and a woman—fliers—on Saipan when she was a girl. The woman, she said, "had her hair cut like a man." Mrs. Akiyama said she was riding a bicycle when she saw a two-engine plane land on the water in the harbor. As she watched the two people who got out, both wearing trousers, both white-skinned, were led away by Japanese soldiers—led into the woods—where she heard shots ring out.

Fred Goerner made repeated trips to the South Pacific to question islanders there. One person reported seeing a woman who matched Amelia's description. She was a prisoner kept in a house the Japanese used for internment on Saipan. Later this same woman died of dysentery. The man who had arrived with her was beheaded.

Another islander recalled hearing a Japanese trader speak of an American woman flier who came down in the water and was picked up by a Japanese fishing boat—which would seem to confirm Jacqueline Cochran's vision years before.

A CBS news team found a considerable number of witnesses all telling similar stories to these—19 in all—people who remembered either seeing the crash-landing on the water or a man and a woman with white skin who were taken prisoners by the Japanese.

Fred Goerner found a grave on Saipan that he believed might be Amelia Earhart's. When the bones were exhumed and brought to the States to be examined by experts, however, they were found not to be hers—or Noonan's. Plane parts brought up by divers in the Saipan harbor after the war proved to be Japanese.

One of the truly tantalizing facets of this search, though, was that U.S. officials either refused to answer Fred Goerner's questions, or they encouraged him without telling him why. Admiral Chester Nimitz, who commanded the U.S. Pacific

Fleet during World War II, told Goerner he was "on to something that would stagger his imagination." Goerner was finally able to retrieve some 16,000 pages of records from six government departments regarding Amelia Earhart's disappearance—and this after officials had insisted that there were no files.

During Goerner's investigation, Claude A. Swanson, secretary of the navy, told Goerner, "This is a powder keg." General Graves B. Erskin, who was commander of the 5th Marine Corps Division on Iwo Jima and who had served in intelligence during the war, was quoted by Goerner as saying, "We did learn that Earhart was on Saipan and that she died there."

Several Japanese told similar stories to those of the Saipanese.

Still no *hard* evidence was discovered that either pilot or navigator was found and imprisoned by the Japanese in 1937. Given the secrecy that Japan maintained about its activities in the Pacific, it is doubtful that the United States could have known at the time whether the Japanese had located Amelia and Fred Noonan.

The official Coast Guard verdict thus still stands: "faulty radio, lack of adequate preparation, the blinding effect of the rising sun."

Other pilots simply figure Amelia Earhart gambled on the greatest stakes of her career—and lost.

Whether one concludes that she ran out of fuel and went down in the ocean, or that she landed on or near an island and was picked up by the Japanese, Amelia Earhart's fate remains a mystery.

After George Putnam died, his widow told one investigator, "It's too bad I couldn't tell you the truth." What truth? And in the 1970s, American pilot Ann Pellegreno flew an airplane similar to the Electra along Amelia's South Pacific course and found it impossible to believe that she "just went down." For people who swore by Fred Noonan's navigational skills, there is no explanation as to why he failed to find Howland Island.

Shortly after they vanished, a lone memorial light was erected on Howland Island. The plaque there reads:

AMELIA EARHART
1937

During World War II, the light was shut off. It has since been restored. Once a year the Coast Guard stops by this now deserted island to check on its upkeep. The tower is painted white so that it can be used as a marker for daytime navigation.

Amelia Earhart's life was the American dream come true. Born when there was no such thing as an airplane, she grew up to accept flying as her personal life path. Right along with those "daring young men in their flying machines," she blazed a trail for others to follow. And like those other flyers of her time, she went on guts, instinct, and a lightheartedness that belied the seriousness of her undertakings. Those flyers captured the American spirit of independence and daring—without which no real discoveries would be made.

In her final flight and the search that ensued, much was learned that later became the basis for techniques which undoubtedly saved many lives. Flying to advance the state of aviation, Amelia Earhart achieved this goal to the end.

She started out in aviation because she found it fun. Following that joy brought her to the point where flying became her life's work. However, though hard-driven to stay ahead of a field of fearless female aviators, she still found thrills, satisfaction, and pleasure in flying. It was this enthusiasm that brought her from the state of amateur pilot to professional, tops in her field.

To the end, she especially hoped that the things she did would help young people to find their own ways to keep an enthusiasm for living that in turn would make triumphs like hers possible.

In *Courage Is the Price*, her sister, Muriel, wrote:

> AE loved life every day from the time she slid down the . . .
> home-made roller coaster . . . to the day in July 1937 when she

climbed aboard her beloved Electra in Lae, well knowing the hazards but resolutely facing the odds. . . . I say it was fun having you as a sister, Meely.

Amelia Earhart preferred that her deeds speak for themselves. To honor her is to forget the tragedy of her disappearance and instead remember her for what she did—and what she was.

As Edna St. Vincent Millay wrote,

Take up the song:
Forget the epitaph.

EPILOGUE

What was there about Amelia Earhart's life that we can learn from? What was her contribution to us, to aviation, to herself?

Amelia Earhart's courage is incontestable. "Courage," she wrote in a poem of her youth, "is the price that life exacts for granting peace." She paid the price willingly, even exuberantly. Yet while courage is an admirable quality, taken to excess it is self-destructive; it drives a person on to attempt thoughtless dares, to death.

Part of Earhart's beauty was the fact that she thought of herself as flying on behalf of womankind. In doing this, she blazed a trail for women not only in aviation but in the wide world itself. She hacked out a path that she and others followed in the teeth of male opposition. When men took to the air, their fight was against the machine itself, the turbulence of nature, fear. In their battle for the right to fly, women faced those forces, and one more; they had to fight the men who, with narrow-minded jealousy, thought of flight as a male preserve. Amelia took them on and won. We will long remember her victory.

Amelia Earhart flew on behalf of women; more particularly she flew for all the pioneer women who took to the skies but who remain unknown to this very day, their stories unrecorded. She is remembered in their stead. But the light on Howland Island burns not just for her; it burns for them too.

To understand Amelia Earhart, we also need to understand the age in which she lived, and the spirit of that age. "I'm gonna live forever! I'm gonna learn how to fly!" epitomizes the dream of aviation's pioneers in the early twentieth century. One of humanity's ancient ambitions was finally realized. To this cause, men and women in the 1920's were prepared to devote everything they had, including life itself. Amelia Earhart symbolizes that commitment.

Earhart died as she had lived. "Don't go!" we want to yell, as she and Noonan take off in the Elektra at Lae, New Guinea, July 2, 1937. They move toward their destruction; we are helpless to interfere. We are wiser than they, but also not so wise. All that we are left with are questions. What happened to them? Where did the fliers vanish? Is she really gone?

APPENDICES

APPENDIX A
Amelia Earhart's Flight Around the World at the Equator
Second Attempt: Ports of Call
(in chronological order)

Oakland, California (takeoff)
Tucson, Arizona
New Orleans, Louisiana
Miami, Florida
San Juan, Puerto Rico
Caripito, Venezuela
Paramaribo, Surinam
Fortaleza, Brazil
Natal, Brazil
St. Louis, Senegal
Gao, Mali
Fort Lamy, Chad
El Fasher, Sudan
Khartoum, Sudan
Massawa, Eritrea
Assab, Djibouti
Gwadar, Pakistan
Karachi, Pakistan
Calcutta, India
Akyab, Burma
Rangoon, Burma
Bangkok, Thailand
Singapore, Malaysia
Bandung, Indonesia
Surabaya, Indonesia
Kupang, Indonesia
Port Darwin, Australia
Lae, New Guinea
Lost near Howland Island,
   South Pacific

APPENDIX B
Amelia Earhart's Flight Career (by date)

1920   Learned to fly, soloed after approximately 10 hours

1922   Set altitude record for women, 14,000 feet, Long Beach, California

1928   (June 17-18): First woman to cross Atlantic by airplane

1929   (November 22): Set women's speed record, 181.18 mph

1931   (April 8): Ascended 18,415 feet in autogyro

1932   (May 20-21): First woman to solo Atlantic by air, in 14 hours 45 minutes, a transatlantic record; first woman to cross Atlantic twice by air

1932   (August 24-25): Established women's transcontinental nonstop speed record—Los Angeles, California, to Newark, New Jersey, in 19 hours 5 minutes

1933   (July 7-8): Broke own transcontinental speed record to set new women's nonstop distance record, flying Los Angeles to Newark, New Jersey in 17 hours 47 minutes

1935   (January 11-12): Honolulu, Hawaii, to Oakland, California, first person to solo the Pacific Ocean from Hawaii to California; first person to accomplish flights over both oceans; first person to solo anywhere in Pacific

1935   (April 19-20): First person to solo Los Angeles to Mexico City

1935   (May 8): First person to solo Mexico City to Newark, New Jersey

1937   (May 17): Set record for east-west crossing: flying, Oakland, California, to Honolulu, Hawaii, in 15 hours, 52 minutes

1937   (June 1-July 2): Around the world at the equator.
Two stops from completion of her journey, Amelia Earhart vanished.

APPENDIX C
Amelia Earhart's Honors & Awards

Cross of Legion of Honor, France
Insignia of Order of Leopold, Belgium
Order of Aviation Merit, Rumania
Gold Medal of National Geographic Society, United States
Distinguished Flying Cross, Congress of the United States
Lindbergh Medal
American Society of Mechanical Engineers Medal
Society of Women Geographers Medal
Le Lycéum Société des Femmes de France of New York, Medal
Harmon Trophy, 1937 (with Jean Batten of Australia)
Lafayette Flying Corps Medal
Women's Roosevelt Memorial Association Medallion
Columbia Broadcasting System Medallion
City of New York Mayor's Committee Medal
City of New York Medal of Valor
City of Chicago Medal
City of Philadelphia Medal
Commonwealth of Massachusetts Medal
City of Toledo Medal
City of Buffalo, Key
City of Toledo, Key
Kansas Commonwealth Club Medal
Boy Scouts of America Medal
City of Medford, Massachusetts, Medal
Atlantic City, New Jersey, Key
City of Pittsburgh, Key
Ciudad de Mexico Medal
Amelia Cardenas Medal
Sociedad Mexicana de Geografia y Estadistica Medal
Le Comité France-Amerique Medal
Aero Club Royal de Belgique Medal

Amelia Earhart was a member of Zonta, International (an organization of executive women in business and professions), which gives an Amelia Earhart graduate scholarship yearly in aeronautical engineering.

BIBLIOGRAPHY

Following are some of the best primary sources of information and material on Amelia Earhart. At Cambridge, Massachusetts, the Radcliffe College Schlesinger Library's collection has papers and photographs that pertain to Amelia Earhart and her mother, Amy Otis Earhart. Details may be located in Volume 9 of *Radcliffe College: Arthur and Elizabeth Schlesinger Library on the History of Women in America, The Manuscript Inventories, Catalogs of Manuscripts, Books and Photographs.*

Purdue University Library, West Lafayette, Indiana, special collections division has documents, photos, maps, scrapbooks, decorations, awards, and some personal memorabilia, including a flight suit, helmet, and goggles. The collection is organized around each historic flight, with particular emphasis on the last round-the-world attempt. A listing of what is available may be obtained from the library.

The Medford, Massachusetts, Public Library has some photos, letters, and written material in its archive collection that may be seen by appointment.

The National Air and Space Museum at the Smithsonian Institution in Washington, D.C., has many books, photos, and some unpublished manuscripts, including a taped symposium from 1982 at which AE's sister, Muriel Earhart Morrissey, spoke. They will supply a lengthy bibliography and resource guide on request.

The International Women's Air and Space Museum, Inc., in Centerville, Ohio, director Nancy Hopkins Tier, has AE memorabilia and papers as well as material covering other early women fliers.

The Ninety-Nines, Inc., International Women's Pilots Organization, International Headquarters at P.O. Box 59965, Will Rogers World Airport, Oklahoma City, Oklahoma 73159, has much material on AE, as well as on other women in aviation.

The Teterboro Aviation Museum in Teterboro, New Jersey, while small, is worth a visit because of its photo collection.

In the summer of 1987 much material related to AE and her family was moved into her birthplace, the house in Atchison, Kansas, which belonged to her maternal grandparents, the Otises. This home has been turned into an Amelia Earhart museum.

For newspaper sources, the *New York Herald Tribune* and *New York Times* are two of the best.

As for books, the one that gives the most intimate portrait of AE was written by her husband, George Palmer Putnam. *Soaring Wings* (Harcourt Brace, 1939) provides glimpses of her in the heyday of her great adventures, views that no one else saw.

Muriel Earhart Morrissey's book *Courage Is the Price* (McCormick-Armstrong, 1963) captures their childhood days together and addresses their father's alcohol problem.

AE's own books, *20 Hrs., 40 Mins.*, *The Fun of It*, and *Last Flight*, while careful not to reveal too much, do show her humility, her humor, and her tendency to poetry. *The Fun of It* has recently been reissued in paperback by Academy Chicago Publishers, 1984.

Vincent Loomis's *Amelia Earhart: The Final Story* (Random House, 1985) is the most recent investigation and presents an enthralling detective story of that journey.

Another fairly recent publication is Jean L. Backus's *Letters from Amelia* (Beacon Press, 1982). This is a collection of letters from AE's teenage days up to the final flight. Again, AE does not reveal herself deeply in her writing, nonetheless a picture emerges of her almost despite herself. We see her playfulness and dedication to family.

John Burke's *Winged Legend* (G.P. Putnam's Sons, 1970) presents an overall view of AE and can generally be found in most libraries.

Following is a list of books for further reading.

Backus, Jean L. *Letters from Amelia*. Boston: Beacon Press, 1982. A glimpse into the personal life of Amelia Earhart through her letters from 1914 to 1937. Even in her correspondence, she remains an enigma.

Briand, Jr., Paul L. *Daughter of the Sky*. New York: Duell, Sloan and Pearce, 1960. Plenty of details presented here by a good storyteller.

Burke, John. *Winged Legend*. New York: G.P. Putnam's Sons, 1970. Particularly strong on the last flight details and an overview of the world at that time.

Cochran, Jacqueline. *The Stars at Noon*. Boston: Little, Brown, 1954. Few details on Amelia Earhart's life but an interesting portrayal of the life of this famous woman pilot and friend of Amelia, who showed a similar spirit of adventure and daring.

Davis, Burke. *Amelia Earhart*. New York: G.P. Putnam's Sons, 1972. Especially good information on the post-*Friendship* days.

Earhart, Amelia. *Last Flight*. New York: Harcourt, Brace, 1937. Taken from her writeups of the last flight published in the *New York Herald Tribune*, as arranged by George Palmer Putnam.

———. *The Fun of It*. New York: Harcourt, Brace, 1932; Chicago: Academy Chicago Publishers, 1984. A breezy, unassuming book (not long on details) that probably gives more insight into the understated style of Amelia Earhart than any other.

———. "Try Flying Yourself." *Cosmopolitan*, November 1928.

———. *20 Hrs., 40 Min.* New York: G.P. Putnam's Sons, 1928. The quickly whipped-up version of *The Friendship* flight as told through the eyes of its pre-fame star. Clips from Earhart's log en route reflect the poetry and humility that came together in her.

Ferris, Helen. *Five Girls Who Dared*. Freeport, New York: Books for Libraries Press, 1931. A collection of five heroic true-life tales.

Goerner, Frederick. *The Search for Amelia Earhart*. Garden City, N.Y.: Doubleday, 1966. The detective hunt undertaken by this broadcasting newsman who tried to find out what happened to Amelia Earhart and Fred Noonan in 1937.

Gurr, Joseph H. Letter to Frederick Goerner, May 3, 1982. Smithsonian Institution.

Hamill, Pete. "The Cult of Amelia Earhart." *Ms.*, September 1976.

Harris, Sherwood. *The First to Fly*. New York: Simon & Schuster, 1970. A thoroughly entertaining and well-documented look at early aviation pioneers from the Wrights to the barnstormers and wing walkers.

Hooven, Frederick J. "Amelia Earhart's Last Flight." Report presented to Smithsonian Institution Symposium, June 1982.

Lindbergh, Anne Morrow. *Bring Me a Unicorn. Diaries and Letters of Anne Morrow Lindbergh 1922-1928*. New York: Harcourt Brace Jovanovich, 1971. The budding romance of this shy, sensitive girl with a world hero as well as with aviation itself. The future is there to read.

Lindbergh, Charles A. *We*. New York: G.P. Putnam's Sons, 1927. First solo crossing of the Atlantic as described by this famous flier. Included are his views on the future of aviation at that time and how he got into flying.

Loomis, Vincent V., with Jeffrey L. Ethell. *Amelia Earhart/The Final Story*. New York: Random House, 1985. A thriller. What really happened? Loomis tackles the question with gusto and digs up new facts.

Moolman, Valerie, and eds. *Women Aloft*. Alexandria, Va.: Time Life Books, 1981. An excellent collection of data on women in aviation throughout the world.

Morrissey, Muriel Earhart. *Courage Is the Price*. Wichita, Kan.: McCormick-Armstrong Publishing Division, 1963. Strong on the early family days, startling for its honesty.

Oakes, Claudia M. *United States Women in Aviation 1930-1939*. Washington: Smithsonian Institution Press, 1985. A paperback publication available by mail from the Smithsonian, written by its resident expert on Amelia Earhart. It also contains information on many of America's other famous women fliers. A detailed survey, it also provides records and air race results from Earhart's period.

Olds, Elizabeth Fagg. *Women of the Four Winds*. Boston: Houghton Mifflin, 1985. Some fascinating glimpses of hardy risk takers from other eras.

Putnam, George Palmer. *Soaring Wings*. New York: Harcourt Brace, 1939. Some quotes and insights on Amelia Earhart to be found nowhere else. His was the intimate vision that is presented here with affection. This book first revealed AE's note to GP the day of their wedding.

Radford, Paul, Jr. "Amelia Earhart—her own navigator?" Speech given to National Aviation Club, June 17, 1982.

Seibert, Jerry. *Amelia Earhart: First Lady of the Air*. Boston: Houghton Mifflin, 1960. An overview.

Smith, Elinor. *Aviatrix*. New York: Harcourt Brace Jovanovich, 1981. Smith has no time for George Putnam but goes a little easier on Amelia Earhart.

Wisner, Bill. *Vanished Without a Trace!* New York: Berkley Medallion Books, 1977. A collection of "vanished" stories from real life, including a chapter on the Earhart disappearance in the South Pacific. A capsule vision of the event.

INDEX

B 92   Pearce, Carol A.
EARHART
        Amelia Earhart

$16.95   Occ 3721

DATE			
MAR. 13	OCT. 7		
MAR. 27	OCT. 14		
NOV. 18			
MAR. 25	8-16		
APR. 15	1-24-02		
OCT 13	3-28-03		
JAN 31			
FEB 14			
FEB 16			
JAN 25			
FEB 18			
SEP. 30			

Chapter 2
E.C.I.A.-1989

© THE BAKER & TAYLOR CO.